Praise for
The Upside of Digital Devices

D1043549

"Dreiske's strategies for linking lite... screen content are ingenious and child-centered, engaging young screen users as readers. In *The Upside of Digital Devices*, she conveys this important work in ways that are dynamic, informed by years of research, and deeply applicable to us all."

—**Dr. John Cech**, Director for the Center for
Children's Literature and Culture, University of Florida

"I've seen Nicole's simple yet powerful technique in action and know it works. As an anti-bullying speaker and expert, I witness the effect screens have on young minds every day, and this book will save lives."

—**Jodee Blanco**, anti-bullying expert and author of
The New York Times bestseller *Please Stop Laughing At Me*

"Nicole has restaged the light shining on the hidden dangers of technology and consumerism to illuminate the smartest use of electronic devices, the new public health players in the 21st century. She aptly and clearly shows us how to keep from hurting ourselves, our well-being, and our children, by applying systematic principles of healthy screen use to our digital devices."

—**Dr. Nicholas Peneff, PhD**,
President, Public Health & Safety, Inc.

"Nicole is the world's leading expert on how kids can and should interact with media and screens so that they bring their higher order thinking to bear. For every adult who's wondered *how* to talk with young children about digital devices, this is the book that will change the parenting paradigm around screens."

—**Salim Ismail**, founding Executive Director of
Singularity University, bestselling author of
Exponential Organizations, Chair of ExO Works,
and former Vice President of Yahoo!

THE Upside OF DIGITAL Devices

How to Make Your Child More Screen Smart™, Literate, and Emotionally Intelligent

NICOLE DREISKE

Health Communications, Inc.
Deerfield Beach, Florida

www.hcibooks.com

Library of Congress Cataloging-in-Publication Data
is available through the Library of Congress

ISBN-13: 978-07573-2047-7 (Paperback)
ISBN-10: 07573-2047-3 (Paperback)
ISBN-13: 978-07573-2046-0 (ePub)
ISBN-10: 07573-2046-5 (ePub)

Publisher: Health Communications, Inc.
       3201 S.W. 15th Street
       Deerfield Beach, FL 33442–8190

Cover design by Larissa Hise Henoch
Interior design and formatting by Lawna Patterson Oldfield

To Nan Greenough,
with regards, best
wishes and thanks for
all the wonderful things
you do for
Winnetka

To the thousands of children
who taught me to cherish
their humanity, insights,
and compassion.

Nicole Dreeske

Contents

Acknowledgments

People around the world and around the block have contributed to this book and I owe thanks to them all. Happily, this isn't a fancy awards show and I won't be driven offstage by a crescendo of music, so here goes.

The first and deservedly most effusive thanks go to the incomparable Jodee Blanco who not only brought this book to a fabulous publisher, HCI, but guided each step of the book's vision. She's an inspiration and, although much younger and cuter than I, Jodee is the book's "real mom."

Right up there with Jodee in bringing these ideas to their full fruition is my immensely professional "book doctor" Thomas Hauck, who was the first to create elegant order in the chaos of overwritten chapters I sent him. He's the best pilot a first-time author could have in flying and landing a manuscript.

Bob and Usha Cunningham, Jamie and Anita Orlikoff, and Curt Matthews were my best book angels along with my mom, who lent me her lovely lake house for writing. Christine Martin, Carol Meyers, Pam Conant, Jennifer Brown, Kimberley McArthur, and John Cech were all in the supporting choir. Thank you all for making it possible for me to work with Jodee and Thomas to finish this book while running the International Children's Media Center (ICMC)!

Jina Lee, bless you for your early and endless work on transcribing these ideas and for listening to me put the Screen Smart concepts together step by step. Alex Granato, thank you for your long-ago research on topics I wanted to include in the book. Thanks to my inveterate and patient first readers and citation editors, Rocco Thompson and Christina Condei, who labored through constant subhead shuffling to place citations and make meaning.

A special thanks to Doris and Howard Conant, two dear friends and great supporters of the arts and social justice, who have passed on. Doris saw the merit of the book right away and told me to "get a professional to work on it." "I am a professional," I said. "Yes, but the wrong kind," Doris responded. "Get someone who knows how to write a book." So I did.

Because they're mentioned so frequently, I want to thank Chloe and Charlie Dreiske, my niece and nephew, along with tens of thousands of schoolchildren, teachers, and principals whose experiences formed the foundations for screen talk and the Screen Smart approach.

Another shout-out goes to my dedicated and talented core ICMC staff, Michelle Zaladonis, Tess Walker, and Alex Babbitt, who put up with my working remotely over a summer when we had six festivals, a Global Girls residency, and twelve interns viewing eight hundred films.

Neither the book nor Screen Smart would have been possible without the help of Newton Minow and the fine lawyers at Sidley Austin who worked on a pro bono basis for me to obtain the ICMC's nonprofit 501(c)3 status. Undying thanks also to the visionary Seabury Foundation, the wonderful folks at the Polk Bros. Foundation, the T-Mobile Foundation, the Conant Family Foundation, and the Dr. Scholl Foundation who supported the Screen Smart program in its crucial proof-of-concept years.

The final thanks must really go to the filmmakers whose work helps open so many young minds in so many ways. You're amazing, gifted, and caring, and I hope you make many more great films for kids!

Movies really can make you smarter. Who knew?

Preface

In 1996, I screened the film *The Wind in the Willows* for 200 schoolchildren at Piper's Alley theater in Chicago. This latest version of the children's classic featured many Monty Python alumni, and the film's director and star, Terry Jones, attended the packed event. About thirty minutes into the show, a ten-year-old girl came out of the theater sobbing, followed by her teacher. Terry, the good-natured father of two children, spent a good ten minutes talking to this little girl as she was crying. Unfortunately, no soothing or reassurances worked—she simply kept sobbing.

So I took her to a quiet part of the theater, and asked her if she watched television at home. With a little hiccupping sob, she said "No, we're Orthodox. We don't watch any screens at home."

I responded gently, "Your teacher said you read the book, so why does the movie seem so scary?"

She said, "But when you read a book you have a choice about what's in your mind, and when you see a movie you have no choice at all."

That was a call to action for me. It became very clear that even children who are extremely bright and who are avid readers can be vulnerable to screen content in ways that adults can't anticipate or mitigate. I wanted children to know that they have choices. They, like

> I wanted children to know that they have choices. They, like we, can choose what to "let in" to their minds and how to process what they allow in.

we, can choose what to "let in" to their minds and how to process what they allow in. Right then, I decided it might be worthwhile to turn the decades I had spent talking with children about movies into practical strategies that would open the door to real adult-child dialogue about screen time.

I'm someone who's watched thousands of films with children for over forty years. I started the first juried, competitive film festival for children in the United States and got the Academy of Motion Picture Arts and Sciences to recognize it so that short-film winners of a children's festival could potentially compete for the Academy Awards. I've addressed the World Summit on Media for Children and given more than one thousand workshops teaching children to watch movies with their "minds awake," during the Screen Smart program, a twelve-session residency taught in schools, preschools, and social service agencies. In Screen Smart workshops, children learn how to engage with screens as active participants, to notice what they're feeling and experiencing as they're watching, and to process that knowledge for greater self-understanding and awareness. The technique, effective on kids of all ages, didn't develop overnight and wasn't perfected in a laboratory. I'm not a doctor or an academic, though their voices are represented here. I think you'll be delightfully surprised and inspired by some of what they have to say. I *am* an expert on listening to kids and turning screen time into a rich and meaningful opportunity for growth.

When I was giving workshops for the National Association for the Education of Young Children (NAEYC) at the group's national conferences, I heard many parents voice concerns about their inability to talk to their kids about what they were seeing on screens: TV, film, and online. Some would ask questions during the presentations while others approached me after, seeking advice. The same thing happened at children's film festivals after parent chaperones heard me talking before each screening to children about how to watch a screen with your "mind awake." Wherever I went, I encountered more frustrated parents looking for ways to get their children to open up about what they were watching on TV, movies, and on the Internet.

I soon discovered it wasn't only parents who were eager for information on the subject. The Illinois Chapter of the American Academy of Pediatrics asked me to present at their annual conference. They wanted scripts doctors could use with parents on mediating children's screen experiences. They also requested scripts for parents to help them talk with their little ones.

In 2007, I sat on a panel called Critical Viewing: The Game the Whole Family Can Play, chaired by David Kleeman, then the president of the American Center for Children and Media. At the end of the discussion, a parent in the audience stood up. She was emotional and sounded almost desperate.

"These are great ideas," she said. "But where do we start, how do we start, especially when they're tiny?" It was a valid question because toddlers and preschool-aged children have limited vocabularies and attention spans.

At that point, I shared some of the techniques I had developed for an illustrated children's book, *TV Time at My House*. My team and I had been testing the book in daycare centers and preschools for the past few years. I also talked a bit about the methodology behind the techniques. The response was electrifying. Another woman stood up and then another, wanting to know more.

That's why I wrote this book. We have the power to help children "prime" their minds *before* they start

> We have the power to help children "prime" their minds *before* they start watching screens, and approach media as they would a book, with an "awakened" critical mind

watching screens, and approach media as they would a book, with an "awakened" critical mind, looking for themes, characters, and plot. With this easy-to-read guide, I wanted to help parents, teachers, counselors, and childcare providers engage their children, open lines of communication, and lead their kids through the media minefield. This way, kids could learn for themselves how to make safe, healthy choices. Perhaps through this book all of us can even leverage the astonishing power of media to teach and inspire.

Introduction

Do you sometimes rely on digital media to occupy your child because you've had a deeply draining day and need half an hour to catch your breath? Perhaps you were driving your preschooler to an activity and you gave her your iPhone to have a little peace and quiet in the car. You're aware you shouldn't be allowing your devices to become impromptu babysitters, but there are moments where it seems there's no other option. Listen to me: that doesn't make you a bad parent. It simply makes you a very human one.

I'm a realist. I understand the unrelenting demands on parents' time. You're pulled in a million different directions, each one a priority. When you're on the fly, you don't always have the luxury of being able to think through every situation. You do what any over-burdened, well-intentioned parent does—you wing it. Most of us cope the best we can, juggling far too much, hoping we can get through the day having protected our little ones.

Then there's the guilt. Remember that old public service announcement campaign, "Do you know where your children are?" It's as if the slogan has shifted to, "Do you know what your child is doing right now," or more specifically, "what screen your child is using right now?" How often are we bombarded with statistics about children and screen time? Experts on talk shows, blogs, websites, books, and watchdog groups are continually warning already frightened parents that if you don't police the amount of time your child sits with a screen and what they're watching, you're negligent and could be damaging your little one for life. You agonize. You lose sleep over it. You can only be so many places at once. And what if your child is on a playdate at someone else's house? You can ask, but you can't assume those parents will follow your guidelines in their home. Moreover, even if they do, kids can be sneaky about screen choices. As they get older, if they want to watch something, they'll find a way to access it. The questions you have to consider—and I need you to be honest with yourself here—are how much can you really *control* what your child is watching and why do we all focus so much on this particular point?

You can't be with your son or daughter 24/7 and you can't successfully insulate them by enforcing rigid or nuanced restrictions on screen activity. What about the content you approve? Sometimes seemingly innocent programs can have a more negative affect on children than programs the experts tell you to avoid entirely. I can't tell you how many kids have told me that *Lilo & Stitch* gave them nightmares, and that the horror movie they saw made them laugh because it was so "dumb." Narrative content is interpretive and subjective. There's no way to predict how a child will react to something. Yes, you can make an educated guess about your own child's response, and there's a lot of good info out there to help guide you. Ultimately however, no matter how vigilant you are, policing your children's screen time takes a huge amount of effort and emotional energy. Unfortunately, in the long run, it doesn't really get the job done.

So what is the job? Is it primarily protection? If we're trying to help our children develop twenty-first century skills, is it enough to protect kids from screens by keeping them away from "harmful" content and limiting their screen-time exposure? I'm not suggesting you let children watch or play with screens all the time or watch anything they want, let alone watch randomly with older siblings. But no one can simply protect a child from digital influences and call that preparing

children for success in the twenty-first
century. To help our kids become "Screen
Smart," we've got to move beyond protection into preparation.

To help our kids become "Screen Smart," we've got to move beyond protection into preparation.

Here's the great news. You can leave
many of those concerns about policing and protection behind
because you already have many of the tools you need to help your
child truly thrive in the digital world. You're just not using those tools
in relation to screen time yet. So we're going to start fresh, by envisioning the relationship we *want* our children to have with screens,
and then exploring the opportunities within screen time to build that
new and positive relationship.

Sure, we'll look at how screen time is affecting us and our children.
But we'll start from a new perspective. Instead of talking only about
"what they watch, when they watch, how much they watch," we'll
start with the catalyst questions that I asked more than a thousand
parents and teachers:

What would a *great* relationship with screens and technology look
like?

Would you like your children to confide in you when they've been
scared or confused or disturbed or delighted by something
they've seen on a screen?

Would you like your children to know and be able to communicate what they're feeling and thinking about what they're
watching?

Would you like your child to notice that character, plot, and setting aren't just in books, they're also in movies, shows, and
games?

The answers to these questions became a "wish list" that drove
the development of the techniques you'll find in this book. It's just a

matter of deciding what we want out of screen time so we can identify how it can best serve us and our young children.

Although the majority of my techniques are focused on children ages two to six, the basic methodology works for all ages. The language for older children may be more sophisticated, but it's never too late to start learning healthy screen habits.

We'll explore how screen time can become a powerful asset to boost your child's intelligence and social emotional learning. Instead of creating digital cocoons that divorce you from your children, screen time can help you better understand and relate to them. And here's a surprise: it all starts with reading. Great screen-time experiences build on great reading experiences. You already know that reading to children is one of the most important developmental activities you can undertake for a child's success.

Let me give you a little overview about what we'll be doing together here, and I want you to know that none of it will put unrealistic demands on your time. I'm simply going to help you polish some parenting tools you already use, repurpose others, and show you some new techniques for teaching your child how to engage with screens in a healthy way and dialogue with you about it. Up until now you may have felt frustrated when you tried to talk to your child about their screen-time experiences. You may have no idea how to get the dialogue started. Maybe when you ask them a question, they offer a vague answer or go silent. We're going to change that simply by making some small adjustments in how you approach the conversation, the tone and cadence of your voice, and how to properly frame a question to children so they're comfortable enough to open up, and lots of other subtle but powerful strategies. I'll show you how to help your child develop her own internal filters and controls while interacting with a screen. You'll get tips on how to create a positive safe environment for discussion about screen time; how to teach your child about plot, character, and setting; fun and creative ways to build your child's literacy acuity during screen time; how to improve their vocabulary, ability to communicate, emotional intelligence, and higher-order thinking skills through talking about what they're watching, and much more.

I'll also tell you some stories from my work in the field with kids and how they inspired the techniques I'll be showing you. These stories range from festivals to frontline classrooms and family coaching. Some of the little ones you'll meet in these pages will make you chuckle with their remarkable wisdom and honesty. Others will make you appreciate your own children from a whole new perspective. My purpose in including these stories is to reassure you that you're not alone, that every parent, no matter where they live, their economic or social status, religion or ethnicity, shares these concerns about how screens are impacting our children's futures. We are all committed to our children, not only as their caregivers and protectors, but also as their mentors. Screens and digital devices are here to stay. They'll only become more ubiquitous, so we have to march forward with intent, be ready, and get our families ready.

I'm confident you'll not only enjoy mastering the techniques in this book, but, the more you read, the more excited you'll become about trying out all that you're learning. You'll soon realize that you *can* teach your young child to be Screen Smart, and you'll make wonderful memories while doing it. You and your child are about to embark on a life-changing adventure together navigating the digital landscape. I'll provide the survival kit to make that adventure fun, easy, and rewarding. Let's get started!

Chapter 1

Know What Your Kids Are Watching

If you have kids, at one time or another you've probably said this to a friend, relative, or teacher: "Limiting TV isn't the problem. I *know* the limits. But what do I talk about *after* they've seen the show?"

Or this: "My husband and I can't be everywhere and see everything they see. What do we say when they get upset about something that we don't even know about?"

Or perhaps you've said this: "I try to talk to my two littlest about what they're watching, but they don't want to discuss it with me. What am I doing wrong? How do I get them to talk to me? What do I say?"

Sound familiar? You're not alone. What's the problem? Is it that your kids are spending too much time on screens? Maybe yes, maybe no. According to the Nielsen ratings, our youngest children (ages two to five) spend twenty-eight to thirty-one hours a week—between fourteen hundred and sixteen hundred hours a year—with their eyes glued to a screen, immersed in some form of visual content.[1]

While you may think that's too much, the intent of this book is not to argue how many hours of screen time your kids should have. That's a decision for you as a parent, knowing your child and balancing issues like family time, school, and recommendations of trusted advisors like pediatricians. But it can't be denied that this amount of screen time has a significant impact on parenting, particularly when it comes to understanding and interacting with our children. If we don't understand how a child is responding to what they're watching (or playing), then we don't understand that child, because they spend more time with screens than they do with any other activity outside of sleep.

> If we don't understand how a child is responding to what they're watching (or playing), then we don't understand that child because they spend more time with screens than they do with any other activity outside of sleep.

Developing a real understanding of your child's responses during screen time takes skills that you already have. When my niece was seven years old, she was watching reruns of *Buffy the Vampire Slayer* with her thirteen-year-old brother and a couple of his friends in my mother's study. I didn't know what they were watching, but after about twenty minutes she came out of the study with her little brow furrowed, and said, "Auntie 'Cole, when I watch TV with the big kids, I get afraid for my grown-up life."

I had heard her laughing and giggling from the other room and assumed everything was fine. Was I wrong! She needed to talk and she wanted someone to listen. So I stopped what I was doing and walked with her to the porch. There, I started asking questions and listening to her answers.

"What were you watching?" I asked.

"Buffy, and there was killing and screaming. People were scared."

"People in the show or people watching?

"People in the show."

"So you get scared when the characters, the people in the show, are scared."

She nodded, looking forlorn, and I leaned down and opened my arms.

"Would it help if you sat on my lap for a hug?" I offered.

After she nodded, I took her on my lap in the rocking chair, and we started rocking.

"So why do you think the characters in the show were scared?"

"Sometimes no one can help them," said my niece.

"Wow, you're right. It would be scary if no one could help you. But is that true, sweetie? Is it true *for you* that no one can help you?"

"Sometimes at school. My teacher says I'm not smart and no one can help me." *Ouch!* Here I had to wait a beat and absorb what she had said.

"I see why you're scared," I said. "So I'm going to make you a promise. Any time there's something for school or anything else you need help with, I'll help you. Or Grandma or Daddy or Mommy will help you. We want to help. All you have to do is let us know, sweetie, can you do that?"

I'm truly grateful that she came to me and we were able to talk things out; otherwise, I can't be sure how it might have impacted her. My niece opened up to me because she felt comfortable. I paid attention to my approach, tone, and tempo when drawing out the details of her experience, and I genuinely cared about what she had to say.

Chloe's story brings us to a topic that affects many parents. While this book provides many techniques for young children, what do you do when there are big age differences between children watching together? In some families, the access to tablets and smart phones has made this less of an issue because the older children can play games or watch different content on their devices while the younger ones watch age-appropriate content. But for times when the age differences between your young digital natives may still pose a challenge, see special tips in Chapter 13.

Active Listening

So let's look at the bigger picture of adult-child communications. It won't surprise you to learn that the best adult-child communications start with active listening, an accessible skill that turns you into a super parent. Although it's often associated with counseling and conflict resolution, it's a skill every parent needs. Plus, as a parent, with active listening you're ahead of the game from the start because you don't need to take several sessions to learn the trigger points, temperament, and background of your child, the way a therapist would with a client.

> Active listening is a way of listening and responding that promotes shared understanding and builds better relationships.

Active listening is a way of listening and responding that promotes shared understanding and builds better relationships. It starts with the goal of truly understanding the feelings and ideas of the child, something to which every parent aspires. How many times have we listened with "half an ear" and assumed we know what the child is saying? Active listening replaces both those behaviors with a simple strategy that will yield greater closeness and far more effective parent-child communication.

In active listening, you'll want to:

- ❖ Concentrate. Give the child your full attention.
- ❖ Understand. Don't assume you know; listen with an open mind.
- ❖ Respond. While the child is speaking, nod and show your attentiveness, then respond verbally once you've fully understood.

Remember, by tracking the course of the conversation, you demonstrate that you really *were* listening, and your verbal responses will be more specific and effective. The reason it's important to concentrate and understand is so that responding can become a dynamic process. Some of the ways you'll respond will involve:

❖ Summarizing
❖ Questioning
❖ Paraphrasing
❖ Clarifying

I'll include a list of books on active listening, and many of the scripts that I'll include in this book model these steps.[2]

There are many hidden benefits to active listening. For example, it conveys to our children that we value what they say and that we value their opinions, even when those opinions may differ from our own. This is a confidence-builder for children and encourages independent thought. In the "remember and respond" phases, active listening also generates a free flow of ideas, not only facilitating exchange and sharing, but allowing parents and children to appreciate the differences and connections between their ideas. But first we need to be able to get our children to talk to us!

Be Interested in What Interests Them

We can start building the bridge to dialogue with our surly tweens and teens by showing interest in the things that interest them when they're young. Take their first digital journeys with them, not to protect them but to enjoy the experience. If they happen to start *My Very Hungry Caterpillar* with a friend instead of with you, get in and try it yourself and then talk to them! Find out what part of the game they like the best and why. After they've played for a while, start the wheels of dialogue spinning by asking them to talk first, pay more attention to what they're seeing on the screen, and second, reflect on the experience. Here, I often have the child on my lap holding the tablet.

"Why do we like playing this game so much?" The child may shrug, or say, "I like it!"

"So it's fun? What makes it fun? Is it the sounds? The colors? The way the caterpillar or other characters look?"

The next time she plays, I may or may not play with her from the beginning, but I'll focus on helping her get a little self-awareness going. In our dizzying digital world, it's never too soon to develop *metacognition*, the ability to reflect on our own thoughts.

"So how do you feel when you hear the bell (buzzer, music) get louder?"

"It's pretty music."

"I like it, too. What feeling does it give you when you hear it?"

"Happy."

"Is that all? I see you wiggling when you hear the music. Why do you wiggle?"

This kind of interaction lets the child know that you're interested in what they're feeling, and that knowing what they feel and how they're responding is something you want to be part of. Also, these kinds of conversations can go in many different directions depending on the context and conditions. If you're at the airport and your child is overtired, it may not be the best time to try for a deeper dialogue. But it could also be a motherlode moment when your child starts talking a blue streak and putting together ideas. Whatever the situation, always be prepared to say *ELMO*, "Enough, let's move on," instead of forcing a discussion.

Include Them in Adult Conversations

Another way to fast track our children's growth and development is simply to include them in adult conversations. They may not be interested at the start, but parent attention is a pretty potent lure.

So when you're discussing current events with your spouse at dinner or in the car, find ways to include your child if those events are child appropriate. In general, topics such as murders, bombings, wars, child abductions, or how much you hate the current administration are best discussed with other adults. If the child asks you questions about "hot" topics, that's something else entirely. Often, questions about wars, killings, or extreme weather surface because a child is seeking comfort and stability. Here, I'm looking at the best ways of using current events to involve children in grown-up discourse. Neutral or good topics would include successful rescues, elections, budget crises, the opening of a new zoo.

I generally recommend starting this at age four and up, but some children are verbal and interested earlier. You invite inclusion by saying, "Do you know what we're talking about, honey?" Just have a simple synopsis ready to share, in case the child has no clue. For example, "We're talking about the president, do you know who that is?" Trust me, questions will follow, and the child will develop confidence, curiosity, and an appetite for participating in adult conversation.

Children who've been included in adult discourse develop higher-order thinking skills much faster. Here are a few quick examples:

> Children who've been included in adult discourse develop higher-order thinking skills much faster.

An eight-year-old named James surprised me when I asked a class of second-grade students about their experiences with nonfiction media. According to James, "We have to watch the world a lot more closely now. It's changing so fast." James's mom Roberta said that he'd been "part of family talks about world news since he was in preschool."

Ten-year-old Sabrina's pediatrician had been close to her family since they had immigrated from Mumbai. In one of my workshops, he recounted that "Sabrina sat at dinner with eight adults and contributed to the conversation when we were talking about the effects of Reaganomics. It was clear that she was considered an equal—not special or precocious—just on a par with the other adults."

When four-year-old Stacey's parents began letting her ask questions during the 2016 election, they let her form her own opinions. After watching part of a debate, and some opening talks, she came to the conclusion that one of the male candidates for president was "a bully," because of "how he talks and makes mean faces."

(The day after the election, she asked her parents the same question I was asked several times by children in Chicago schools: "If bullies are bad, why did the bully win?")

We need to bridge the gap between these spaces that we've reserved as adults-only to create spaces where adults and children can converse together. When such conversations occur at random, naturally and unforced, the payoff is incredible.

Why We Need Screen Talk

To bridge the gap and end screen-based segregation of adults and children, we also need to check the emotional and energetic vibe we send out when we're using screens ourselves. I'm not just talking about television here. Picture the "don't bother me" bubble you create around yourself when you're working on your phone. Not only do children mimic that self-created isolation, but it's a natural deterrent to starting to talk about screen use.

Cultural and generational experiences also contribute to the segregation of adults and children during screen time. Baby boomers who resisted the old, "Do as I say, not as I do" discipline that characterized a lot of parenting in the 1950s and '60s wanted to do things differently when they became parents.

Some tried to break down the harshness of parental barriers by allowing the permissiveness they had craved and by becoming their children's friends. Others who felt deprived of emotional support may have overcompensated by becoming much vaunted "helicopter" parents who wanted oversight on every childhood experience. I think we've all seen the fallout from that approach.

Family structures like chores and curfews got harder and harder to maintain. But freeing kids from contributing to the family tends to backfire, by elevating resentments on both sides. A couple of decades down the road the kids who were your "friends" can't do anything for themselves and expect you to do it for them.

We're not just segregated from our children by the ways we use screens. The way the media portrays parents and children on popular networks contributed to the parent-child divide. In many popular sitcoms and movies, parents and adults were (and still are) portrayed as foolish or bumbling, while children were portrayed as clever and mouthy. The adult was often shown as impeding the child's growth and creativity and initiative. It seems so benign compared to rampant pornography or graphic special effects that show body parts exploding across a screen, and yet the myth of the ineffectual parent is one of our most toxic twenty-first century cultural legacies.

Current conventional wisdom in parenting encourages balancing screen time with real-time activities like art-making, sports, a walk in the park, or going to the zoo. That's a great first step! Many parents who are aware of the seduction of screens work hard at providing their children with a full range of sensory play and creative and family experiences where they interact outside of screen time. But that strategy effectively segregates screen time from normal family interaction, from communication and laughter and shared experience.

Long term, the segregation of screen time from "real-life activities" is both counterproductive and truly wasteful. That's because the process of making screen time a multisensory, interactive pursuit is not difficult and yields such extraordinary results. I think one problem that parents may face when envisioning "screen talk" or "interacting with screens together" is that we've been assigned the jobs of censoring, selecting, and supervising children's screen time for too long. For seventy-plus years parents have been put in the unenviable position of creating safe-media *prisons* as a means of protecting our children. Who wants to be a prison warden in their own home?

That approach has long since been proven to be flawed because of children's great aptitude in accessing content when they are outside the family home and their great facility for circumventing the kinds of electronic controls that are put into place for anything from the Internet to movies. So preparing children rather than merely protecting them is a very attractive and sensible alternative. Because sooner or later they're going to exit the protective bubble, and the ability to process and select their own screen experiences are invaluable twenty-first century skills.

So preparing children rather than merely protecting them is a very attractive and sensible alternative.

Let's look at these things: the V-chip, apps to track children's screen use, complete parental censorship and avoidance of disturbing material, limiting time spent with screens to an hour a day, and making sure that all extended family and friends observe the same limitations.

Even if you were 100 percent successful with that, at the end of the day, you have children who still have never talked about their screen-time experiences and who don't know how to process confusing or disturbing content. They are still out of touch with the thoughts and feelings that screen content inspires, and they are still spending far too much time with only one side of their brains. The end game for complete success of all parental controls is obedience and overprotection. The end game for what I'm suggesting is creative, independent thinkers who can select the media that is most appropriate for them, question it, and then discuss it with others and have rational, intelligent discourse about the most powerful influences in their lives.

Parents would have to go to extraordinary lengths to achieve 100 percent success in protecting their children, ensuring that they stay safely in their media prisons, and enforcing obedience in viewing choices. Using that same time and energy to develop a relationship with your child around screen time has a far more meaningful outcome and is a much better investment of your time in that child's future.

Screen talk also builds, rather than stresses, family bonds, and the opportunities are endless when you consider the sheer volume of children's viewing hours. Remember those 1,400 to 1,600 hours? Of course, that figure only increases in a child's later years with elevated time on phones, Facebook, Instagram, etc.

I said it before, but it's a question that bears repeating: if your child is engaging in any activity for 1,600 hours a year, and you don't know what your child is thinking and feeling about that experience, how well do you know your child? Even if those 1,600 hours are divided between different kinds of screens, spending that much time viewing without communicating, reflecting, or processing means that media is a one-way street for little ones. Everything goes in and nothing comes out, so pressure builds up in the mind. Talking, thinking, processing, and reflecting help relieve that pressure.

The joys of screen talk aren't limited to children. When a group of adults watches a film and then talks about it together, the experience can be transformative. They're sharing very different ideas, they're learning about things they had no idea their peers thought, and they're observing that other people had a completely different experience from the one that they had. So when I started giving professional development workshops for teachers in the 1990s, I was stunned when 80 to 90 percent of educators said that they had never talked about a film with other adults. Listening to movie experts talk about films can be enlightening and entertaining, and the Turner Classic Movies channel has tapped into a real niche with its informative pre- and post-screening talks. But actually discussing your own ideas and insights with a small group can be a revelation. As one teacher in an International Baccalaureate school said, "Talking about movies taught me about myself and how I respond. If I hadn't talked about my own reactions, I wouldn't have realized that so much was happening in my own mind while I was watching."

Screen talk opens your and your child's mind to new layers of meaning within that content. The ability to make meaning from what we experience is one of our most crucial twenty-first century skills. By not including that as part of education, and as part of family experience, we're not only wasting opportunities, we're also closing doors that need to stay open if we are to have a healthy relationship with screens moving forward. Pediatricians agree![3]

Screen talk opens your and your child's mind to new layers of meaning within that content. The ability to make meaning from what we experience is one of our most crucial twenty-first century skills.

Chapter 2

Watching and Talking Go Together

The first question many parents ask is, "When is the best time to talk to my child about what he or she is watching?" The answer is, "At the moment they're watching the movie!" That's right: watching and talking go hand in hand.

Collective family discussions aren't necessary every time your child watches a screen. Several times a week are enough! That way there will be enough interactive, parent-bonding experiences around screen time to help children overcome the expectation of being alone with their screens. Of course, this is going to play out differently depending on the child's age, temperament, and preferences, including whether the child is introverted or extroverted. But this idea of talking to your children around screens is like a perfect gift that's never been unwrapped.

The optimum age to start screen talk is based on your child's verbal and emotional development. You're the gateway to healthy screen habits, and to teach those your child has to be verbal and mature enough to listen and respond. Short answer: you start screen talk at the age when your child can communicate verbally and you allow her to look at screens.

Talk During the Movie (Is That a Thing?)

To get the ball rolling, it's beneficial over the course of a week to watch a few short programs with your child, encouraging dialogue with open-ended questions *during viewing*. I'll provide several examples of the kinds of questions I use with children later in this chapter.

I can hear you screaming, "But I just got Angie to sit still and watch a whole feature film in a theater without talking!" Don't worry—you won't erase all your earlier efforts to get your child to watch movies in relative silence. You can simply divide movie viewing into two categories by saying, "Sometimes we talk during the movie and sometimes we wait to talk. Today we're going to . . ."

But while you're working hard to teach your child the many benefits of sitting still and being quiet, please know that watching anything that's seventy- to ninety-minutes long is the opposite of what children ages two to six need developmentally, physically, and intellectually. I'm all for self-regulation, but if I'm watching a feature film with a very young child the best possible thing would be to get the child talking while she's watching it. Especially if the movie shows things that are the opposite of all of the other developmental and family values we're trying to impart.

In workshops, parents often tell me that they want to start a conversation with their children, but they don't know how. When they discover how much fun it is and how easy it is, they're sometimes puzzled about why they didn't make the connection before. Not to worry! Baby boomer and Gen X and millennial parents may have grown up with different screens and have had different formative experiences with technology, but we're all the same in one respect: no one ever talked to us about our screen experiences, so it doesn't occur to most of us to include screens in family dialogue.

Even when parents recognize that the stories on screens and the stories in books have a lot in common, it doesn't quite feel natural to start talking because there are layers of learned behaviors around screens that take precedence.

From the 1940s through the 1980s, people sat with television sets, and if you talked during TV time, Dad would yell at you. If Mom's on her cell phone, you don't bother her. You're supposed to be quiet in a movie theater. Art-house cinemas are sometimes quieter than libraries! So don't blame yourself if you haven't been talking to your kids about or during screen time. Often, our culture and behavioral patterning hasn't fully supported "screen talk" before now.

One of the finest educators I know, Dr. Emilye Hunter-Fields, contradicted that. "Nicole, you need to go down to the South Side movie theaters in Chicago and sit with some African-American audiences. Our folks talk back to the screen and react verbally to foreshadowing. They'll tell that fool to move out of the way, or warn that girl to leave some no-good criminal."

When traveling through parts of North Africa and South America, I noticed the same thing. People from many different cultures talked to the screen in public while a film was playing. I found it refreshing, although I could certainly understand why other movie-goers may have found it annoying.

Watching films at home with scores of different families, I noticed great differences in screen-time behavior and interactions. Some families "shush" each other and generally prefer silence during screen time, while in other families, adults spoke to or about characters on the screen during the program. Some of these differences were due to the quality of the program or the general level of focus and attention in the room. But denouements, "big reveals," and moments of high drama or emotion generally commanded greater silence around the screen, often followed by verbal or nonverbal responses. Interestingly, more than 80 percent of the young people I've interviewed tell me that they "yell at the screen" when the story is overly predictable or characters are TSTL (Too Stupid To Live). So the "code of silence" may not be as hard to break as we think.

In 2013, at Walt Disney Magnet School, a highly regarded school on Chicago's North Side, I was approached by a parent after the screening we usually hold for families at the end of the Screen Smart program. She had watched the children do the priming exercise and had seen the excitement that they brought both to viewing and to discussing a) what was on the screen, and b) their responses to it. Her first words to me were, "I wanted to meet the person who ruined my daughter for watching feature films."

She had been very pleased when she had finally trained her four-year-old daughter to sit still for the ninety- to one-hundred twenty minutes required to view a feature film. I do not doubt that that is a skill, and I sincerely applauded the mother for having taught her daughter so successfully. I hasten to add that in a public theater viewing of any feature film, the skill of sitting still and watching will be much appreciated by the parents and children close to you. But every screen context is different, and viewing at home affords numerous opportunities for enriching the child's understanding of what can happen during screen time. Those same opportunities don't exist in most public spaces, nor am I recommending that you undertake all of the techniques I'm offering in this book in those contexts.

I told this very alert and supportive parent that the process of engaging a child in ways that will encourage her to think independently and creatively starts in early childhood. And if the activity that they spend more time with than any other activity outside of sleep involves screens, it may be in the child's best interest to develop the fullest possible complement of awareness, thoughts, structures, categories, and communications about screen content with people whom they love and trust. Positioning screen time as a rarified, energized, intimate activity in which children can explore stories and their own minds will make screen time truly magical.

Having them sit silently while watching screen content *empowers the creators (and sellers) of that content.* It accords the creators of that content greater importance than we, the audience, and places the content itself above the child. That creates a lifelong tendency, as I said in the last chapter, to *follow* rather than *lead,* and to honor the creative output of media makers over their own potential creative expression. In early childhood when formative experiences carry so much weight, we want to start the child's relationship with screens with experiences that allow them to infer and learn that we are superior to and in charge of the technology we use. Technology and screen content exist to serve us, not drive or dominate us. The understanding that "what happens in your mind is as important as what happens on the screen" will serve our children well as they move forward in a world populated by artificial intelligence (AI) and virtual reality (VR).

The mom and I parted on excellent terms and what she said was, "Wow, so watching screens can be like taking them to the library."

Here, I am not suggesting that parents replace trips to the library with screen time. Although, in the 1970s and 1980s, I confess to agreeing with Groucho Marx when he said, "I find television very educational. The minute somebody turns it on, I go to the library and read a good book."

Still, enriching screen time with the story-infused approach of library time is a fantastic recipe for building neural networks and communication skills. Screen time is not a substitute for trips to the library, or for reading aloud to a child and encouraging her to read on her

Whether you're watching a You-
Tube video together or guiding
your child through a new app,
you can use digital devices in
the same way that you would
use story time: to build trust,
emotional intelligence, literacy,
and communication skills.

own. But whether you're watching a YouTube video together or
guiding your child through a new
app, you can use digital devices
in the same way that you would
use story time: to build trust,
emotional intelligence, literacy,
and communication skills. In
this way, screen time can become
a dynamic "whole child" growth agent that will leaven your child's
learning the same way that yeast causes bread to rise.

As adults we'll probably continue to respect the cultural mores
that adjure us to silence while watching cinema or live theater. But
we're going to break that code of silence around screens for our kids.
They, and we, need the closeness, the confidence, and sense of community that comes from talking about their experiences.

Most important, we want them to confide in us because communication is the key to a healthy family. We adults need to pull in our
prickliness about talking during screen time, swap our "don't do that"
voices for our "story-time voices," get down to the child's eye level
with a smile, ask questions, and listen to their answers. This simple
recipe for engagement yields an endless cornucopia of discussions.
Better yet, children will start confiding in adults instead of turning
to the four-year-old next to them and saying, "Huh? What do you
think of this?"

Sensory-Friendly Screenings

Recognizing that there are different viewing styles and needs,
many libraries and some commercial theater chains have started
offering what they call *sensory-friendly screenings* or *sensory movies*.

At a sensory-friendly screening, the lights in the theater remain on and the sound is turned down but not off. Although the policies for sensory screenings may differ somewhat from venue to venue, most audiences are free to move around the theater, jump up and down, or talk to the screen.

Sensory screenings were initially programmed for individuals on the autism spectrum for whom a friendly environment is one with a manageable amount of sensory stimulation. The diminished stimulation helps them remain calmer and better able to relate to others, and process the stimulation they're receiving. But sensory screenings aren't just helpful to children on the autism spectrum. In suburbs throughout the Chicago metropolitan area, families with toddlers and pre-K age children are enjoying sensory-friendly screenings where fidgeting and speaking are acceptable. Also, if your child is extremely sensitive to the bright lights, special effects, and high sound levels that characterize the majority of commercial screenings, sensory screenings may be a perfect solution. Plus, you can practice your "screen talk" right there in the theater! A quick search of sensory screenings or sensory-friendly screenings will turn up what's available in your area.

The Right Time for Screen Talk and Co-Viewing

Picking the right time for "screen talk" will occur to you naturally. It can happen in the middle of the day, it can happen before, during or after mealtime, it can happen during a drive, it can happen during a walk, it can happen in any transitional period, or it can happen as part of "This is what our family does every Friday night." Having a specific time when your children can anticipate screen talk can be very exciting. But the minute it becomes rote, shake up the process and change the schedule.

Learning to talk with your child about what they're watching is best done during co-viewing.

Getting your kids to talk to you (about screens or anything else) will *not* happen if you send the message, "This is when you have to tell me everything that you're thinking."

Learning to talk with your child about what they're watching is best done during co-viewing. Co-viewing is a term that might sound like off-putting jargon, but it's really just a short way of saying, watching screens with your kids. Talking with your children *while* they're watching will teach you how they respond to different kinds of content and how to interject questions, just like learning when to jump in during double Dutch. There's a rhythm to viewing and talking and you'll feel it.

Once you start asking kids questions while co-viewing or co-playing an electronic game, you'll have a much better idea about how to talk to them about shows they've seen or games they've played on their own. You can set aside a morning once or twice a week where you'll see content no more than half an hour long. That's how quickly you can ramp up.

Going into this process, most parents have had some volatile interactions with their children on the topic of screens, usually around time limitations or content choices. Every time you sit with a child and really engage them in co-viewing or co-playing, you are effectively neutralizing the prior negative interactions you've had with that child on that subject and replacing them with new memories, habits, and experiences. At this point, you want to show your child how much fun they can have talking with you when you're relaxed, emotionally available, and curious. In these discussions you, the parent, lead and prompt with open-ended and specific questions, and demonstrate sincere interest in the answers you receive.

Parent Attention Time— Getting to Know PAT

> For the growing psyche of a child, there is nothing more nurturing than a parent's attention.

Let's look at some specific examples of how to create welcoming environments that create fertile ground for screen talk. A lot depends on the rhythms of the family day and the demands of everyone's schedules. There are certain times in the day when a child can get Mom's or Dad's attention, and other times when they can't. For the growing psyche of a child, there is nothing more nurturing than a parent's attention. In balance, giving children our positive attention is the source of every good thing. Even if the time is limited by our availability, it has a great effect on our children, especially if it's predictable and they can count on it. A very elegant IT specialist once told me, "We had a really large family—fifteen siblings. But knowing that I would have 'Mom time' every day gave me confidence and stability and the heart to care about everyone else. Even when I had to share my parents' focus, I knew I had their full attention for those special times, and that made all the difference."

I have friends who work two jobs, and still save time for anything kids want from Mom or Dad, whether it's cuddling or complaining. "Sometime between dinner and getting ready for bed, anything goes. They know I'm theirs for fifteen minutes."

Of course, parent attention time (PAT) can change. In some families, it floats to different days, but always at the same time. Having it at the same time every day or evening gives children something stable to look forward to. Each family finds its own way to signal to their children that it's a good time for parental attention.

But here are a couple of tips. Unlimited PAT that's on offer to children 24/7 isn't in your or the child's best interest. They need guidelines and ground rules that teach them to value your time and distinguish it from their own. Recognizing that people are separate from you and have their own needs is part of the normal process of maturing.

Introducing PAT when your children are tweens requires a different approach. A casual, "Anything you want to talk about, sweetie?" won't open that door if you've never opened it before. For sure, they're going to say "No," or give you the eye roll. But there is a way to get those eleven- to thirteen-year-olds and even seventeen-year-olds to talk with you. Just demonstrate real interest in the things that interest them. You've probably been doing this with your littlest children all along. For example, if your child has an interest in art, and you know that he loves to draw, you can talk about his drawing after he's finished or sit with him while he's drawing, watch, and ask questions. As always, our tone should never be intrusive or demanding. Just be positive and expectant, or quiet, in keeping with the child's mood and focus:

> "Is this an animal?"
> "Yes, a cow."
> "Where'd you get the idea to draw a cow?"
> "From milk."
> "So, what's the green thing in the sky?"
> "The sun."
> "The sun is green?" Because I raise my eyebrows and look surprised, there's some giggling.
> "Yeah, the sun looked green through the leaves when I was hiding in the bushes."

When you're genuinely curious and you start asking specific questions based on prior active listening, your child will start telling you fanciful and fascinating things that invite you to share the way they relate to their world. Studies show that creative play is one of the wellsprings of emotional and mental growth in childhood. Showing interest and engaging the child verbally during or after play will leverage the experience, prompting greater self-awareness, and emotional and intellectual development.

Family Movie Nights

One of the easiest ways to make screens part of family time is to set up family movie nights. Nell Minow's *The Movie Mom's Guide to Family Movies* offers an excellent overview of classic children's films, together with tips for starting discussions. It may feel old school, but you're actually creating the experience of going to the movies in your own home. Bill and Melinda Gates did it regularly with their children, and they're certainly not Luddites.

Family movie nights also broaden the screen-time experience to include the family as a whole rather than just one parent and one child. But it's more than just sitting on the couch with popcorn and watching something together. It's your entrée to a dialogue that will allow you access to the magical corridors of your children's minds. Even if you haven't had great talks with your kids before, movies and family viewing can be your ticket in!

Pause and Question, aka P&Q

In the classroom, when we're focused on accelerating the learning process, we rarely show a film all the way through. We're also familiar with the films, but even if you're not fully familiar with programs your child is watching, you'll notice many moments to use the remote control. Pausing the film at first may seem intrusive or even annoying. But look at it this way—when you're reading a book with your child, don't you pause now and then to comment on the action? Does this ruin the experience of the book? Of course not—it *adds* to it.

> Rise above the bias against pausing because giving your child the chance to fully notice details and connect to what they see on the screen can enhance everything from kindergarten readiness to advanced literacy skills.

And aren't TV shows full of commercials that interrupt the narrative, often in the most annoying places—typically just before a climax or resolution of the dramatic tension? Of course they are! Even the youngest children are accustomed to interruptions from commercials.

Rise above the bias against pausing because giving your child the chance to fully notice details and connect to what they see on the screen can enhance everything from kindergarten readiness to advanced literacy skills. It's just too juicy an opportunity to ignore. The process of framing questions during a screening depends on using general, simple vocabulary, and the ability to quickly rephrase the question if the child does not understand the first time. The rephrasing should be positive and playful, not judgmental of the child's ability to understand what you've said.

Here's an example. One of the first films I screen in the Screen Smart program is a charming CGI (computer generated imagery) film called *Cuckoo for Two* by directors Angie Hauch and Angela Tidball. The opening of the film shows a room that an adult might identify as an office or a living room with a cuckoo clock on the wall. The style is imaginative and detailed in ways that suggest to an adult viewer that what you are about to see may be fiction or even fantasy. In the opening shot, we pause the film and ask the children what the setting is, and ask them to point out and name the different objects in this room that would tell them what the setting is.

The second time we pause the film, we focus on the different photographic portraits that the director has placed on the wall in the room where the story takes place. In every one of those photos, there are two people who appear to be a couple. The questions that we ask are very simple: "Who do we think those people are? Why would their pictures be on the wall? How many people are in each photograph? Who do we think those people are to each other?"

Very young children will answer each of these questions quite differently. Most will be able to infer that photos are of the people who live in the house. It's also evident that there are two people in every photo, and letting the child notice and "own" that observation is a confidence-builder.

Often the last question will prompt answers that the two people in the photo are a couple, friend, that they like each other, that they are boyfriend and girlfriend, that they are married, etc. There is a broad range of answers, all of which confirm that there's an emotional connection between these two people. The very next shot is of the cuckoo bird in the clock looking down and sighing. We stop. First, we ask the question, "How does the cuckoo bird feel?" Every child can identify that the cuckoo bird feels sad. If we want to focus on emotional intelligence, we'll ask the children to point out the visual details that show how the bird is feeling. Then we'll ask about the cause of the emotion.

"Why do you think the cuckoo bird feels sad?"

Usually even two-year-old children will be able to answer: "The bird is alone and he looks lonely." But sometimes they're so young that they're not practiced at making inferential connections yet. So an appropriate cue would be, "In every single photograph that we've seen on the walls, how many people were there?" They'll remember that there were two people. To make things more interesting, add a little counting game into the viewing, I may stop, rewind, and count all the photographs. Then we know that there are eight photographs.

"So in eight photographs, we saw two people in each photograph. How many cuckoo birds are there?"

They'll look and say, "One."

"So why do you think the cuckoo bird is sad?"

The children will answer, "Because he's alone," "Because he's lonely," "Because he has no friend." (Again, there will be many different kinds of answers.) What has happened is that the child's knowledge base has been affirmed at every step of the questioning process by allowing him to notice and respond and confirm what he's noticed. Then when I ask a question that requires inferential reasoning and emotional intelligence, they are able to go the extra distance.

Another opportunity for "P&Q" occurs a little later in the same movie when the cuckoo bird has extricated himself from the clock and is standing on the ledge beneath the clock's door. He is looking at this "lady love," a purple toy bird sitting on a desk approximately 8 feet from the cuckoo clock. The character gives another deep sigh and looks forlorn. I'll pause the film there and ask the question, "Now why is the cuckoobird feeling sad?"

The children have already seen the relationship evolve between the toy bird on the desk and the cuckoo bird on the clock. They know that the cuckoo bird wants to reach the purple bird. Asking the questions allows them to put together all the data and evidence they have accumulated and make assertions:

"Because he wants to be with the purple bird."
"Because he misses the girl bird."
"Because they can't be together."
"Because he can't fly to her."

Children are extremely receptive to the pause-and-question method as long as you remain encouraging and interested in their answers.

Children will answer in many different ways, and many, if not all, of those answers will be correct.

Children are extremely receptive to the pause-and-question method as long as you remain encouraging and interested in their answers. That is not to say that 100 percent of them easily make the transition from sequential viewing to P&Q. In a classroom, it may take 10 percent of the children a couple of sessions to get used to the process. But please remember: I'm not suggesting that parents use the P&Q approach every time for everything their children watch. However, it's easy to introduce when playing an electronic game or using an app with your child because there are many places where the games and apps pause. Those provide great opportunities to point to the screen and interact with your child, asking questions that are not only constructive but fun to answer!

I get extraordinary outcomes doing this for half an hour once a week in a school setting. In the home setting, I would recommend ten minutes three times a week at a minimum to build the observational and communication skills that will drive the development of inferential reasoning and higher-order thinking. It will also acclimate you, the parent, to a fuller enjoyment of your child's brilliance as a digital native.

> In the home setting, I would recommend ten minutes three times a week at a minimum to build the observational and communication skills that will drive the development of inferential reasoning and higher-order thinking.

In schools, at the conclusion of the Screen Smart program, parents are invited for a final screening event to celebrate children's Screen Smart skills. At this screening, I show all the films viewed during the program, and parents are frequently amazed at the insights and responses their children are able to offer.

Following one such screening in 2014, the father of a three-year-old girl was interviewed. His daughter had talked to him extensively about the movies she had seen in the program. "The big thing I noticed is that Charlotte is incorporating the vocabulary from the films into her everyday language," he said. "Also, she was so excited about one of the films that she came home and told me and my wife all about it, and when we went to the family screening it was exactly as she described it."[1]

Watching Tumble Leaf and Fig

Let's look at how parents can interact with children during and after screen time. Here, I'll share a dialogue with a child while co-viewing an award-winning pre-K program called *Tumble Leaf*, produced by Bix Pix Entertainment for Amazon Studios.

The main character of *Tumble Leaf* is a character with a blue face, named Fig.

Fig is a fox and he has lots of friends, from hedgehogs to turtles to fish. The series is filled with imaginative settings and charming characters all beautifully designed. There is always a special puzzle for Fig to figure out. Before starting the show, I invite children to watch with me in a special way.

"While we're watching, let's think about what we like, what we don't like, and why. Can we do that? Let's say it together. What we like, what we don't like, and why." (I make it fun for kids to say those words with me, by inflecting up and using gestures as I speak. We call this "priming" and I'll talk more about priming in Chapters 8 and 9.)

"Okay, so I'm going to ask you questions some of the time, and you can ask me questions, too!"

From the beginning, there's an underlying feeling of playfulness. It shows children that this is something we're going to be doing *together* that's as enjoyable and active and interactive as any other kind of play. We're raising the bar for what "fun with screens" feels like. Good co-viewing is going to *feel like* (not replace) going to the zoo and asking questions and talking about the animals and finding out more about them.

So we've primed with, "What do we like, what don't we like, and why," and let children know that we can ask questions throughout. It's helpful and fun to have a remote that allows you to stop and talk. This is where the magic starts. Within the first 90 seconds of co-viewing, I start asking questions:

"What is this setting, Jenny? What do you think that setting is?"

And if she says, "I don't know what setting is," I stop the film and say, "Setting is where and when the story takes place. Let's say that together. Where and when the story takes place." Even (and especially) when giving kids important vocabulary, I inflect up to emphasize the fun factor.

You've not only laid a foundation for discussing what's going on on the screen, you've also given your child a huge advantage on the literacy track. If your child goes into pre-kindergarten knowing plot, character, and setting, she has a big advantage when it comes to reading skills. Sitting with your child during screen time brings all the essential ingredients for learning together in one place:

> If your child goes into pre-kindergarten knowing plot, character, and setting, she has a big advantage when it comes to reading skills.

1) Physical proximity, closeness with a beloved parent
2) A parent's undivided attention
3) A cherished activity: screen time

Kids love watching screens and they're visual learners. So if you're talking to them and engaging them with your love, support, and interest, your outcomes are going to flourish. In this example, I asked the first question about the setting, but that question could just as easily have been about the characters and what they're doing. What we want to do first is get children comfortable with answering questions that prompt them to notice details and that introduce the vocabulary used to talk about stories. Setting is one of them.

Then I might pause at a very clear shot where there are three characters onscreen, and I would ask, "Jenny, how many characters are on the screen?"

If she goes right to counting, and says "three," you've just learned that your child already knows the word "character," so you can build on it later.

If she asks, "What are characters?" or says, "I don't know what characters are," you get the chance to tell her!

Here's an efficient way to introduce character: "Characters are the people, animals, or things in a story or a movie. Let's say that together! I'll say it, then you say it." (To help your littlest ones, you can point to yourself when you talk, and point to them when you want them to talk.)

Characters are (Characters are)

The people (The people)

The animals (The animals)

Or the things (Or the things)

In a story or movie (In a story or a movie!)

"So how many characters are on the screen? Want to count them?" Always allow the child to participate and, in a best-case scenario, *lead*. So if Jenny wants to count each character, let her. If she sees three and knows there are three characters, that's fine, too.

There really are no wrong answers when co-viewing because you're on a mission to share personal insights and experiences that can never be "wrong." You don't know what you're going to find, you don't know where the path will take you, but you'll make many discoveries along the way. We think of responses as good, better, best.

> There really are no wrong answers when co-viewing because you're on a mission to share personal insights and experiences that can never be "wrong."

"Okay, so we have three!"

If it took more than a minute to get to that answer, I'll press play and keep watching before asking another question. If the child already knows the word character and quickly identified that there were three characters, I might throw in another question right away.

"Wow, lots of colors. What color is Fig's face? What color is his kite?"

Toward Sensory and Social Emotional Learning

Eventually we get to a point in the story where Fig can't figure something out, and he'll take a deep sigh. You stop the film, and you mimic the deep sigh and say:

"That's a *sigh*. When someone sighs (sigh), how do they feel?"

Children may answer: tired, sad, sorry. Whatever the answer, you now have a choice. You can move on with inferential reasoning or you can go a different direction toward emotional intelligence, helping the child make a text-to-self connection.

To connect with emotional intelligence, you simply ask the child about her own feelings when she did what the character on the screen was doing.

"How do you feel when you sigh? We were at the grocery store and you sighed when I said we wouldn't buy candy."

"I was sad."

"I was disappointed."

"I was mad at you" (complete with frown and arms crossed) These are just some of the answers you might get.

At that point I continue, "But yesterday when I asked you to bring me your shoes, you *sighed*. How did you feel when I asked you to bring me your shoes?"

Although you *may* learn something new about what your child was feeling, the real point of the dialogue is to prompt the child's awareness of his own feelings and practice identifying and talking about them.

Here's another way that same dialogue may unfold. You stop the film, and you mimic the deep sigh and say, "What did Fig just do?"

"He took a breath."

"Yes, but why? Why did he take a breath? What's happening in the story that would make him take a breath?"

Then the child will have to think back to what just happened in the story.

"What was he doing?"

"Well, he was looking for something and he couldn't find it."

"So when he took the deep breath, what did his face look like? Do you remember?"

Remembering and understanding facial expressions is a key competency in developing emotional intelligence. Sometimes children remember, and sometimes you'll need to keep prompting for details.

"Did his eyebrows go up or down?" (They went down.) "If someone's eyebrows go down, how do they feel?" (Make a face with your eyebrows down.) "If I look at you with my eyebrows down, what does it mean? Do I look happy?"

"No, you don't look happy."

"How do I look?"

"You look sad."

"So maybe Fig is not feeling happy. When he sighs, how do you think he's feeling? What is it telling you?"

"That he's feeling sad; he wants to give up!"

There can be a range of responses, and depending on what response you get, you can ask another question, or keep playing with the screen talk. After a longer discussion, I usually let the show or movie play, sometimes pointing out things and asking questions while the program runs. "Has the setting changed?" or "Why do you think Fig is doing that?"

Then, I'll pick another sense to explore. "Do you hear the

music—why is it going faster?" Paying attention to the music can be one of the most effective parts of screen talk, whether you're watching a program or playing with an app. For example, when a character is trying to figure something out, the music is quite different than when the character is celebrating, or annoyed. The music changes all the time. Here's your "neuroscience can be fun" tip for the day. By switching senses, you activate a different part of the brain. This helps your child start building a whole new neural web during the discussion. In effective co-viewing, the child is getting visual stimulation, intellectual stimulation, auditory stimulation, and physical stimulation from cuddling or close proximity to a caregiver. By using questions to lead your child's awareness in varied sensory directions, you keep the co-viewing experience fresh, full, and well-rounded. This is true when you're playing apps and games as well.

> In effective co-viewing, the child is getting visual stimulation, intellectual stimulation, auditory stimulation, and physical stimulation from cuddling or close proximity to a caregiver.

So, what kinds of questions can you ask? Using key words like character, plot, and setting, you can ask questions about:

Colors. What color is that character? What color is that hat?

Shapes. What is that shape? What shapes do we see here?

Numbers. How many pigs are in the picture?

Sounds and sound effects. What sound did we just hear? What could make that sound?

Music. Did you hear how the music changed? What is it telling us? Did it change how you were feeling?

Dialogue. Why did the mom say that?

Feelings. How do you think that character is feeling? Why? How did his face change?

Plot. What just happened? Why?

Sequence. You told me you liked the hedgehog. Did we see the hedgehog at the beginning, the middle, or the end of the movie?

Setting. What is the setting (where the story takes place)? Have we seen something like that before?

Characters. What is the character wearing? How has she changed? What we like, what we don't like and why. What did you like about the program? What did you like? Why?

Audiovisual media has a lot of moving parts. Movies, shows, games are a feast for the eyes and ears. Make the most of that diversity and you'll stimulate your child's enormous powers of retention, attention to detail, inference, and interpretation. If you *only* ask questions about the characters, it will get predictable and preachy and—you're right—the child will get bored.

> But good media contains enough rich and interesting content to support scores of questions moving between visual, interpretive, emotional, and critical thinking.

But good media contains enough rich and interesting content to support scores of questions moving between visual, interpretive, emotional, and critical thinking. The question-and-answer dynamic is much like playing an instrument. Each question is a chord, and as you continue co-viewing, it becomes a sensory and developmental symphony supporting a higher level of learning and enhanced neural networks.

In this chapter, most of the examples have shown the pause-and-question process, but as I suggested earlier, asking questions and getting answers while the program is running or while playing a game works well, too. You can start by pointing out details yourself and ask the same kinds of questions that you'd ask if you paused the film. In continuous co-viewing, I also make sure the child knows that commenting is a two-way street. A gentle, "Hey, you can tell me things you're noticing, too!" generally does the trick.

A quick insight about questions from the child. Although I always let children know they can ask me questions, I rarely answer. Sneaky, I know. Instead I turn the question back to the child saying, "What do you think?" Co-viewing isn't about sharing *my* skills as a media expert; it's about exercising the child's own powers of perception and reasoning. It's about creating an environment for your child to access skills they have but often don't know they're using. More important, you'll find that 90 percent of the questions can be answered by children themselves, outside of the heart-stopping ontological and philosophical questions like, "Grass comes back after it dies, Mommy, why don't people do that?"

When co-viewing, the narrative, the character development, the music, the dialogue, and the plot will lead your questions.

> When co-viewing, the narrative, the character development, the music, the dialogue, and the plot will lead your questions.

It's actually quite a natural process because you've got thousands of hours of experience and expertise yourself! You'll find yourself charting a beautiful dialogue through the course of watching ten to twenty-two minutes of well-produced, early-childhood media.

For the bulk of co-viewing or co-playing, I find it most valuable to select traditional narrative rather than educational content that already contains child-directed cues and navigational buoys that are attempting to fill the gap of an adult co-viewer. Buoys in children's content take the form of title cards, direct-to-camera instructions to children, or voice-overs telling the child what to do. Those devices are there so that a child can watch a show and get learning outcomes when watching by herself. Those programs are best used when you'll be talking with the child after she watches. Prime the expectation of talking, let your child watch by herself while you're taking that last call from your boss before dinner, and then take a couple of minutes to talk about the things she noticed, learned, and liked.

Game On!

You can do this same process with games. Wherever you find characters, colors, settings, objects to count, or actions to discuss, you can engage in dialogue and ask questions during or after playing electronic games. But despite the increasing number of hours spent with apps and games, you'll find that young children are truly most affected by stories. Remember, when you take the time to discuss a media text that has a story, you're also helping to prepare your child for pre-K and kindergarten. You are creating a body of positive memories and experiences with narrative frameworks, and that can only help improve learning.

Again, these experiences are formative, and at the beginning, it's good to dedicate a little more time. You would want to co-view and "pause and question" three times a week or "prime-and-discuss" any solo viewing or gaming.

Chapter 3

Creating a Safe Environment to Talk

Next on our list of screen-time fundamentals is creating a safe place for your child to talk about what they're watching. To start, this means avoiding both interrogation and rebuke when it comes to talking about screen experiences.

It's an unpleasant fact that one of the most contentious realities in many households today is the struggle around screen time. Even in the best-intentioned families there can be an air of inquisition about what programs kids are watching and what games they're playing. It's good to remember that kids don't like to feel interrogated at any age, and early childhood is particularly formative and sensitive. You're laying the foundation that will support or stress communication with your child for the rest of both of your lives.

Let's look at a quick example of how to get back on track if you stray from inviting dialogue and veer into interrogation. Perhaps you found yourself growing anxious because you suspected your child was hiding something from you, so you started bombarding her with questions. It's human nature—you're fearful, so you escalate. Unfortunately, pressuring a child usually elicits a response that's the opposite of the one you're seeking. If you raise your voice and dig in like you're trying to get to the bottom of something, you become an inquisitor. Your child may shut down.

At this point, instead of just stopping or backpedaling, you can redirect the interaction to reestablish emotional ground. Try smiling gently, touching her hand, and referring to something that happened that morning or the evening before: "Hey, you had some bad dreams last night. Was school okay today, or were some of the dreams still in your head?" Including specific information that only you as the parent would know personalizes the question and makes the child feel validated and understood. It's not a lot of effort. It's just a more intuitive—and effective—way of connecting with your little one.

Now let's consider how to handle the tempting impulse to rebuke children about screen experiences. Kids don't like getting in trouble. So they try to avoid it by being "good" or attempting to hide the evidence if they've been "bad." How often has your child begged you to watch something and you've said "No," only to find out two days later that he saw it at his friend's house?

You have two choices. You can get angry and punish him, or you can use it as an opportunity. That doesn't mean you won't discipline him in some way for disobeying you; it means that even though he knows he did something wrong, he still feels comfortable and safe enough to talk about it. So take a few deep breaths, use a gentle, calm inflection, and ask him simple questions about what he watched, like, "Was it scary? What happened in the story? What parts did you like? What parts didn't you like?" After you've had an open, honest exchange, then you can tell him you're disappointed he did something he was told not to do, but you're very proud of him for talking to you about it now.

No matter what, you want an environment in which your child feels safe enough emotionally to confide in you about their experiences even when that includes something they believe may invite punishment. This trust is particularly important to cultivate in relation to screen time. You can deal always with obedience issues later, but

No matter what, you want an environment in which your child feels safe enough emotionally to confide in you about their experiences even when that includes something they believe may invite punishment.

if they're more afraid of *you* than the potentially damaging content to which they were exposed, you'll have a bigger problem in the long run. In this chapter I'll walk you through, step by step, how to create that safe environment, starting when your child is very young. For now, I want to continue familiarizing you with the fundamentals of how the Screen Smart method works.

Ask Open-Ended Questions

Open-ended questions are the secret ingredient in all successful parent-child dialogues. An open-ended question is designed to prompt a meaningful answer based on the child's own knowledge,

Open-ended questions are the secret ingredient in all successful parent-child dialogues.

experience, and feelings. Closed-ended questions merely encourage short or single-word answers. Let's look at some other potential opportunities you can explore for engaging in screen talk. Even an average day can be chock-full of them! You have to work on a Saturday, so your five-year-old daughter goes out with the trusted parents of a friend to watch a film that you approved. She comes home, and, partly out of guilt over your own busy schedule, you pepper her with questions, beginning with, "Did you like it?" Once again, you're an inquisitor.

Young children often shrink from rapid-fire questions. Pay attention to her body language. You may see visible signs of her shutting you out. She might look down or away, begin fidgeting, or start to squirm.

"Did you like it?" is a yes-or-no question and may only yield a nod or a headshake. Remember, caring, specific questions elicit engagement. Also, keep your questions simple and give them as much context as possible. With a younger child, you were probably present for the playdate, so reference the setting.

Let's look at an afternoon playdate for your kindergarten-age daughter. For example, you may say, "You went over to Amber's house this afternoon. What did you play? Did you have any fun?"

She may tell you, "We played Angry Birds and then we watched TV."

For many parents, that's where the dialogue ends. If a child says, "We watched TV," the parent rarely asks *what* they watched. I recommend coming up with a series of open-ended questions that you can rotate and tailor to prompt discussion. Such as:

"Oh? What show did you watch?"

"You played Angry Birds? Did you get many pigs?"

Please note the second question, about the number of pigs defeated in the game, presupposes that you have some knowledge of the video games your kids are playing. Oh, you don't know anything about the games your kids are playing? If that's the case, put down this book and ask your kids to show you the games they play. And then, if you're not afraid to lose to a four-year-old, try playing along with them.

> What they know is how to manipulate technology along desired paths. What they *don't* know is how to decode the messages they're receiving.

Your child is already an expert at using digital devices. Everyone is calling this generation of young children "digital natives." That makes it sound like they really know what they're doing. What they know is how to manipulate technology along desired paths. What they *don't* know is how to decode the messages they're receiving. That's where you, the parent, need to take the time to make talking about screen time a positive family habit, something they grow up with and automatically do with you, like a hug when getting home from school or reading a storybook together at night. Once you establish this practice as the norm, it will revolutionize your child's ability to navigate hurdles, think for themselves, and activate their own filters should they be exposed to inappropriate content. While we always want to protect our children from seeing something they shouldn't, the best form of protection in the digital world is preparation for the unexpected.

Encourage the Sharing of Expertise

Another positive parent-child dynamic that you can leverage is that kids love to make their parents proud. Just think of all the times you've been at a swimming pool or playground when you heard a little one yelling, "Mom, Dad, watch this!" Your child's natural impulse to share what he's learning presents a wonderful opportunity for getting him to open up about his screen experiences. Set up the conversation so that he feels like he's demonstrating his expertise as a screen watcher, the same way he does when he's begging you to look at the sandcastle he just built or how far he can throw a Frisbee.

Kids enjoy being asked their opinions. If you're talking about a game your daughter played or a show your son watched, use language that makes them feel that you value their thoughts and *wait* for their answers. They want the grown-ups to see how smart they are. For example, if your child has watched *Thomas the Tank Engine*, you can ask, "What happened when Thomas got lost? How do you think he felt? How did *you* feel when Gordon saved Thomas from the flood? Why do you think he said that? What was special about what Gordon did?" If you don't know who Thomas and Gordon are, you may want to put down this book and ask your child to explain them—and the other main characters—to you. It's a charming series that teaches many valuable life lessons.

Close Observation Leads to Discovery

Increasing attention and memory skills will boost a child's ability to compare and contrast. With nothing in the memory vault, they have nothing to compare or contrast anything to. Some of the more advanced skills will open to your child naturally without painful remedial steps if you acclimate them to this kind of real-time response.

So I opened by discussing setting, but let's use another example where we're inculcating, rather than instructing, the use of vocabulary used to discuss stories. Back to character, plot, setting. What I first do is have children tell me what color the character is and what the character is. When the cuckoo bird first comes on screen, I will ask, "What is that?"

"That's a bird!"

"What color is it?"

"It's green!"

"Is it a real bird? Does a real bird live inside a house on a clock?"

"No."

"What is it?"

Some children will have seen a cuckoo clock and they'll say, "It's a cuckoo bird!" Others will say it's a toy bird. Others will say it's a real bird. So then we must observe further to find out if the bird is real—I never just correct the child. So we pause at a point where the metal hinge that is on the bird's shoulder is clearly visible. We'll point to the hinge on the bird and ask, "What is that? We see something on the bird's shoulder. What is that?"

They may not know. If they're very young, they may think it's a kind of decoration. Then I'll ask them, "What do you think it's made of? Is it shiny?"

"Yes, it's a little bit shiny."

"What is shiny in the room that we are in now?"

"Oh, things that are plastic are shiny."

"Well could it be plastic? It could be plastic! What else could it be?"

"It could be metal!"

"Okay, so it could be plastic or it could be metal because it's shiny. Is it one part or does it have more than one part?"

They look at the hinge onscreen and see it's in two parts, and they see there are little screws and indentations in it. I let them tell me all the little details they notice.

"So it does something. What do we think it does?" Children will tell me that the metal piece "lets the bird move his wing" or "helps him fly."

At that point, I may want to introduce a new vocabulary word. "Let's pretend I'm the green bird. I don't have a real shoulder. I have metal or plastic right here." I raise my arm out to my side like a wing, and then put it down, placing my hand on my shoulder where the hinge is on the bird. "You told me that this part helps the bird fly and move. Without that part, the wing wouldn't be connected to the bird. It would fall off! Do any of you know the word for a joint that connects two things?"

Often one child will know the word, but if no one knows the word, I'll walk to the door, open it, point to a hinge, and say, "What is this called?" If no one knows, I'll give them the word. "This is a hinge! That's a new word for us. Let's say it together: hinge."

This would be the process I'd use with a class of students. We call it a "scaffolding set," in which we look at an object and develop a series of questions interspersed or overlaid with examples drawn from the film and life lessons. At home, I would point to it and probably simply instruct the child and give them the word "hinge." Then I can ask this question: "Have you ever seen a hinge on the wing of a real bird? Do they have hinges?"

"No, Mommy, birds don't have hinges!"

"So then if a real bird doesn't have a hinge but the bird we're looking at does have a hinge, is that a real bird?"

"No, that's not a real bird. It's a toy bird!"

"Right!" The child then knows that what's going to happen in this story will be tinged with fantasy, because if the main character isn't real, there's a good chance that the whole story will be pushing the boundaries of credibility. But that doesn't mean there aren't scores of "real" teachable moments within that same story.

Chapter 4

How to Talk—
Your Tone Matters

Many of us miss opportunities to engage in real dialogue with our children for one simple reason: we're communicating with them in the ubiquitous, practical ways that take precedence on a daily basis. Typically, adult/child communication falls into one of two categories.

1) **The directive.** We tell the child to "do this" or "do that," and we give them guidelines to follow.

We say, "It's time to do your homework."

"You need to eat your peas."

"Stop hitting your sister."

"Please stop talking. Can't you see Mommy's busy?"

"Don't run near the pool."

When delivering directives, our tone of voice may reflect annoyance, emergency, frustration, and our general desire to control the child's behavior. None of those tones will work for encouraging disclosure and most will firmly close the door. So in general, except for high-energy body movements

51

that come later in the book, the directive tone and approach
are absent from Screen-Smart skills.

2) **The perfunctory check-in.** This is when we try to get a finger
   on the pulse of the child's activities. With a child in elementary or middle school, we may ask them general questions
   about their day, for example, "So how did your day go?" or
   "What did you do today?" Then we feel exasperated if the
   response is a disinterested shrug, or an "I don't know." Sometimes we get such responses because we've asked generic
   questions that don't address the child as an individual. They
   lack context. The more generic you are when you communicate with someone, the more dismissed they feel. The more
   engaged you sound and the more you tailor your questions,
   the more validated they feel. If someone casually asks me
   how my day went, I'll often avoid answering. I'm not motivated to elaborate because the question feels empty, imper-
   sonal, as if there's no genuine caring or concern attached. If
   that same person were to reference something specific, like,
   "Nicole, I know you've had a lot going on with your family,
   how are you doing and how are they?" then I'd be more
   inclined to engage with that person.

Think about the last time someone inquired how *your* day went.
Did you feel that the person was truly present and in the moment
with you, or did it seem like he or she was asking out of polite obli-
gation? When your child gets home from school, are you sometimes
distracted and multitasking when you ask about their day, barely listening when they *do* answer? We all do it, but if you think your child
doesn't pick up on that, you're wrong.

In literature we have flat characters and round characters. Flat
characters are the ones no one remembers and who are only there

to move the plot along. Round characters are the stars of the story. They're written with vivid detail and depth. They're the ones you track, and you want to know what happens to them.

When you ask your child a question, make him or her feel as if they're the star of their own story. Stop what you're doing, look them in the eye, and try to be as specific as possible: "How are you feeling, Amy? I know your tummy was feeling kind of yucky when we walked to school. Did you still like story time? What story did your teacher read you today?" Just as with an adult, you cannot give children platitudes and clichés and expect a meaningful exchange.

> When you ask your child a question, make him or her feel as if they're the star of their own story. Stop what you're doing, look them in the eye, and try to be as specific as possible.

We live in a world of advertising slogans and verbal shortcuts. If you're using one-liners with your children that don't relate to their reality, they're going to tune you out. If most of your verbal cues hover between instructions and perfunctory questions, you're denying yourself the opportunity to know your child more deeply. You may believe they don't want to talk to you, but that couldn't be further from the truth. They're just smart. They know when they're being *talked at* instead of *engaged with*, heard but not listened to, and forced into a conversation rather than approached with empathy.

Your Tone:
Invite Communication

When communicating with your child—or anyone, for that matter—the *tone* of your voice can mean the difference between opening communication and getting the door slammed in your face.

Drawing children into a conversation starts with a welcoming tone that inflects up at the end of sentences. Varying both speed and tempo while talking is also ideal for holding the attention of toddlers and preschool children. For example, if you're speaking in a level tone and your child is losing interest, try lowering your volume or even whispering to regain his or her focus. At other times, a child may need an extra burst of energy with a smile from you to engage them. But if your tone is too coddling and syrupy sweet with a child past the age of three, he's likely to feel babied and may ignore you. Of course, if you speak in a monotone, he'll know you're just getting the question out of the way.

Yes, your child senses when you're on automatic pilot and merely going through the motions. Tone and tempo are akin to body language. Though subtle, both are powerful indicators of sincerity, and little ones especially internalize insincerity even if it's not the message you wish to send.

I recommend tapping into your "storybook voice." How would you read a book aloud to a child? You wouldn't overact the characters, nor would your delivery be stale and flat. Your cadence would have a mellifluous quality to it and you'd probably read with enthusiasm to pique your child's interest. You can incorporate that same warm and inviting timbre when you talk to your child. I'm not suggesting you become overly self-conscious and monitor every syllable. Simply practice the technique of *self-listening*. When you're speaking to your little one, ask yourself, *Are my body language, the sound and rhythm of my voice, and my demeanor all saying, "I acknowledge you as a person"?* Mindful communication is about training your ear to notice how you come across to others and using empathy as your guide to make adjustments in supporting the interaction.

A friend of mine complained that when she was younger, her mom's voice always sounded shrill and angry to her, even when her mom was in a fairly good mood! One day she accidentally recorded her mom, who had come in and spoken to her during violin practice. When my friend was listening to her practice session later, her mother happened to hear her own voice and came in to listen. Her mom was crestfallen when she heard how she came across but then began paying more attention to her tone and inflection. She learned how to step back and *hear herself* during conversations with her children. It took time, but after a few months, the entire dynamic in their home changed, and my friend, now in her fifties, still laughs with her mom, who recently turned eighty, about that day she accidentally (and fortuitously) recorded her voice.

Your Tempo and Body Language

Just as your tone needs to invite communication, so does the tempo of your engagement. How often have you said to your child, "Tell me what happened—*right now!*"? You may even have scowled or stamped your foot for dramatic effect. Chances are, the response you got was a flood of tears from your terrified child and no useful answer. By insisting that your child open up *right now*, you probably got the opposite of what you wanted.

The key is to relax and take your own deep breath or count to ten before you start talking so that you know you're not running roughshod over your own best communication style. If you're rushed, your child will sense that you're not giving him or her your full attention, or that you're stressed. If you're too slow, the child may feel you're condescending. For a deeply personal conversation about feelings, slow and steady will help you gain your child's trust and confidence.

For introducing new ideas, and "teasing" out children's insights, I like to vary my speed, sometimes using a fast, energy-building pace, and at other times slowing down for greater intimacy in the communication.

Nonverbal Communication

In his seminal 1972 book, *Nonverbal Communication*, professor Albert Mehrabian established that 93 percent of adult communication about our likes and dislikes is nonverbal. Since approximately 50 percent of the screen-talk approach encourages children to notice, then share and reflect on their likes and dislikes, Mehrabian's insights are relevant and meaningful.[1]

In nonverbal communication, our posture, the space between ourselves and our child, our breathing, and especially our faces convey information. Movements of the eyes, nose, eyebrows, and mouth express a flow of feelings and impressions. But let's keep it simple. To keep your "nonverbals" supportive during screen talk:

❖ Sit, kneel down, or bend down to the child's level, without looming over them.

❖ Make eye contact.

❖ Put a gentle smile on your face.

❖ Tilt your head to indicate you're listening.

Making these simple physical changes also helps me to stop and give the child my full attention, the first step in active listening.

Articulation Games—Plosives

To keep things lively, make the most of screen talk, and make enunciation fun, I use fast-paced consonant exercises in a technique I call *interdisciplinary scaffolding*. What a mouthful! If you're a teacher you already know about psychologist Lev Vygotsky and his development of the terms "scaffolding" and the "zone of proximal development" (ZPD). Thankfully, it's not necessary to head off on an academic tangent, although I've provided a cheat sheet on Vygotsky's work for those who are interested.[2] What's more important is that these techniques and practices are embedded in screen talk and they're part of every dialogue I've shared with you thus far.

Interdisciplinary scaffolding involves giving the child a challenge and then supporting and coaching her through that challenge to a near-adult level of success with that challenge. Viewing media and playing games offer many opportunities for practicing pronunciation: the title of the program, words included in the dialogue, pop-up vocabulary words all contain surprise packages for practicing speech.

To open those packages, I teach children a high-energy series of inner mouth calisthenics that support consonant production. They're called *plosives*. Plosives are created by pressing the relevant surfaces of the tongue, the lips, the teeth together with a lot of energy (thereby generating a certain amount of muscular resistance) before propelling the sound out using a big breath.

Some of the commonest and most beneficial plosive patterns are: P-T, B-D, K-T, G-D, M-N-NG; F-V-TH.

I use them because they're amazingly effective for improving articulation skills, breaking down speech impediments, and building children's confidence in speaking. Let me give an example. In a screen-talk session, we'll often use the word setting. Even while defining setting ("where the story takes place"), I pay attention to a child's enunciation. If I can barely hear the "t" in setting, he hasn't made a mistake, he's given me an opportunity to scaffold learning! I'll start by asking him to repeat the word.

Then I might tease him and say, "Hold on, I think we lost our T sound. Did it fall on the floor? Let's look!" We'll actually play for two seconds, looking at the floor.

"Nope, no T's on the floor. Okay, let's learn how to make the T sound." Together, we'll touch the tips of our tongues. Then, I'll say, "Put the tip of your tongue in back of your front teeth and *press.*" I'll make the T sound sharply, using a lot of volume: T, T, T. Then, I'll ask children to make the sound with me.

If I don't hear clear T sounds, I'll say, "First let me show you. I'll do it, then you do it. Ready?"

It's a bit challenging to fully describe consonant articulation within the confines of printed pages, but if you do that with a lot of energy, you're exercising the whole mouth and using the specific musculature that supports the production of that T sound. Any word is fair game and fun to "plosivize." Character, plot, and setting each have strong consonants that can be repeated as plosives. The titles of films, games, apps, and TV/YouTube programs offer infinite opportunities for practicing specific consonants and then immediately using those sounds to articulate the words of the title. If a child tells me that she's had trouble pronouncing her own name, we can play with the plosives in her first or last name as a consonant booster.

Plosives aren't taught as a stand-alone; they're part of the whole co-viewing tool kit (or "scaffolding set") that I use to energize children and give them auditory and kinesthetic stimulation before quickly redirecting focus back to specific details on the screen. They're a powerful tool for energizing learning, for exercising pronunciation, and for reducing and alleviating strong accents or combating the problem of infantilized speech.

The cuteness factor of a precocious eighteen-month-old who innocently turns Th to D and R to W can also turn adults to mush, triggering verbal and nonverbal signals of approbation. Who's immune to cuteness? But if, at age seven, your child is getting teased for talking like Elmer Fudd and Mike Ditka combined (e.g. "What's da pwobwem, Mommy?") doing a few plosives while reading or co-viewing can be a great help.

When I handed my five-year-old niece a fork at dinner one evening, everyone thought it was adorable when she said, "Tanks fo da foyk." But I had heard from my brother that some of the other children at her new school were making fun of the way she spoke. They had previously been living on Long Island and she had picked up the accent in less than a year. Impressive! But it can hurt to stand out as "the new kid."

So I gently asked, "Chloe, can you say *fork*?"

Again, she said, "Foyk."

I asked, "Would you like to know how to say *fork*?"

When she nodded, I held up four fingers and asked, smiling, "How many fingers am I holding up?"

"Four."

"Yes, that's right, four!"

Then I drew the letter K and asked, "What's this?"

"K."

"Well let's make that sound!" Plosive hint: inside your mouth, make a small mountain with your tongue. The middle of your tongue will press hard against the big hard bump on top of your mouth. If you're not sure where it is, touch the hard part at the top of your mouth with your thumb. That's the hard palate. So you press your tongue there really, really hard and then drop your jaw, letting the mountain go. Let's do that again. Press. Release. Now *puff* air through at the same time you drop your jaw, and you blow air through, pushing from the diaphragm. So we made the K sounds and did it three or four times.

Then I went back and said, "Let's say that again. Four."

"Four."

"Now the K sound.

"Kuh."

"Now let's put it together: four, *kuh*."

After less than three minutes, she said, "fork." It was powerful not just because of the "correct" pronunciation but because her ear was then attuned to the new sound. Three weeks later, I called and Chloe answered the phone.

She said, "Hello, this is Chloe."

I said, "Chloe, that was wonderful, you answered the phone so beautifully!"

In a flash, she said, "Fork!"

Plosive techniques make self-directed change fun and achievable for children with strong accents, and for children with genuine speech impediments.

Moving forward, she was able to hear and change the accent that was attracting unwanted attention and teasing from her classmates. Plosive techniques make self-directed change fun and achievable for children with strong accents, and for children with genuine speech impediments.

Chapter 5

Fun, Bad, Sad, Scary

If you're two or three years old, how do you tell your parents what's bothering you about things you've seen during screen time? Children need simple vocabulary that allows them to sort their experiences into categories and talk about them. In fact, the process of categorizing promotes the development of neural networks and memory. Whether your child is precocious or barely verbal, don't worry about the simplicity of the language I'm suggesting. Kids are smart. Learning the four words—*fun*, *bad*, *sad*, and *scary*—is like learning that you need to put four corners on your first Lego building. Kids don't stay with the four corner approach for long. Soon they're building imaginative structures that express whole new sets of ideas. The same thing will happen with the first words you give them to help sort their screen-time experiences. They'll build on the simple categories, using new nouns and adjectives to enrich and elaborate on these categories in no time.

I first started thinking about these categories while watching films with the Chicago International Children's Film Festival Children's Jury and Selection Committee. I had allowed some first- and second-grade children to participate in our selection committee and I was little concerned because, at that time, the committee saw, unfiltered, everything sent to the festival. Of course, film synopses and age recommendations made it possible for the committee chair to suss out potential problem films and reserve those for viewing by adults. But there was still a risk that a child might be exposed to disturbing content or to content that made them feel uncomfortable.

Years later, at the International Children's Media Center, I formed all-child film juries, called ICFilmKids. The ICFilmKids saw the films that had been provisionally approved by adults and rated them for enjoyment, originality, and creativity. I wanted children on the ICFilmKid juries to have comfortable, familiar words that spoke to their emotional experiences and their critical thinking experiences. The categories of fun, bad, sad, and scary made it possible for very young children to participate in the ICFilmKid groups along with much older children. Scanning the film synopsis, I used those words to prepare children and invite them not to watch. This was always done gently, by using the words "may be" or "might be." I would take the younger children aside and say, "This movie may be a little scary." Or, "It seems this movie may be a little sad." If they didn't feel like watching something sad, bad, or scary, they could opt out of that particular movie.

So instead of focusing on great ways to tell our kids to turn off screens, I started by engaging children as intelligent, thoughtful viewers who could eventually make good decisions in choosing content for themselves.

Fun

With most emotionally charged topics, and with screens in particular, I think it's important to start with the positive aspect of the experience because, if you start with the negatives, your child is likely to infer that you think this screen stuff is all bad. In fact, many kids already think that we adults don't like what they watch, and they're sensitized to our disapproval *before* they start ignoring our opinions. If you want to build an ongoing, open-door relationship where confidences are exchanged and real dialogue takes place, you need to start positive and establish common ground.

If you want to build an ongoing, open-door relationship where confidences are exchanged and real dialogue takes place, you need to start positive and establish common ground.

Together with groups of three- and four-year-olds, I looked for the simplest word that would encompass why we watch screens, play electronic games, and see movies. Why *do* we watch these screens? Because they're boring? Because we don't like them?

No. Because we think it's *fun* to watch and play with the screens.

And screen experiences that are fun are meant to be enjoyed. They entertain, true, but the best of these screen offerings are also characterized by a good story, good special effects, relatable characters, or other critical film components. And children have the capacity to notice and communicate about all the aspects of media that make something "fun." So the first category that we open up as we start a dialogue with children is "fun." We start by talking about all the things we've seen on screens that are fun, and what, specifically, is fun about them. It's a broad topic and kids get into it, especially if you're interested in what they have to say.

Bad

Moving on to bad, sad, and scary, these three viewing categories were developed to correspond, in the simplest and most memorable way, to the values that parents are communicating and the feelings that troubling content may engender. First, the terms contain both a rhyme and alliteration that make it very easy for young children to retain.

During the development of these terms, when we discussed bad, we knew there were two kinds of bad. The first is when characters are doing something bad or something bad happens. That's the clearest kind of "badness" for very young children to identify. There is also the kind of bad that means a badly made movie. A badly made movie can be one that is unprofessional and embarrassing to watch, or it can be boring. It can also be bad in the way it's constructed. But very young children don't progress to the critical assessment stage until they've had a chance to sort their viewing experiences into categories and start to compare and contrast. So when we first use the word *bad,* it's in reference to things that characters do.

Children know when they've seen content that shows actions and behaviors their parents don't want them to do. They know when they hear things that their parents don't want them to say. It's very easy for them to point the finger and say, "That's bad." It's the perfect opportunity to add, "Are we going to do that?" "No, Mommy, I'm not going to do that!"

But often they won't notice bad unless we give them the opportunity and time to do so. You may be thinking, "Why would I want my child to notice actions and words that are bad? Shouldn't I just direct their attention away from those topics?" First, it's important to remember that most early childhood content shows bad "lite," not adult-level bad. It may involve tricking someone, borrowing without asking, or laughing at someone. If you want your children to be discerning viewers who understand messaging, it's important for them to notice and talk about those messages. More important, if you want children to internalize your positive instructions, their noticing when characters do bad things and affirming that they know not to do those things reinforces your positive parenting.

If they don't notice and discuss the bad content, if that bad content parades by without remark or processing, it can become normative by default.

If they don't notice and discuss the bad content, if that bad content parades by without remark or processing, it can become normative by default. Haley, the frustrated mom of a lively three-year-old, gave a good example: "Over one month, when she was frustrated by her first days in preschool, I must have told Jenny fifty times, 'We don't hit.' But she kept pushing or hitting other children during open play. I knew she would sometimes watch over her seventeen-year-old brother's shoulder while he was playing WoW (World of Warcraft), and I caught her getting up at night to sit on my husband's lap while he was watching wrestling. I didn't think it mattered! But after your workshop, I asked my son to move his computer to his room, and told my husband he couldn't snuggle with her during wrestling matches on TV. She stopped hitting within a week!"

I think Haley's story points to the numbers game implicit in parenting versus screen time. If you tell a child "Hitting hurts, we don't hit" ten times, but during other viewing or gaming experiences they've seen hitting on screens a hundred times without consequences, the hitting wins out. In the formative years, repeated viewing experiences influence behavior, and if those viewing experiences are never discussed, they remain unprocessed. What happens when children consistently see content that demonstrates the opposite of the core positive parenting that caring adults in their lives are trying to provide?

When we were beta-testing the first version of my book *TV Time at My House* in daycare centers, I had the chance to ask many children this question. Here's how it went:

Nicole: "Do your mommy and daddy tell you things like, 'We should share,' 'We should be nice to each other,' 'We shouldn't hit or kick'?" Most children responded affirmatively.

Nicole: "But remember you told me that you see things on screens that Mommy and Daddy tell you not to do. What are those things called?"

Children: "Bad." "Naughty." "Mean." "No no's."

Nicole: "So if you see lots and lots of things that are bad, how does it make you feel? Remember, there is no wrong answer."

Sarah: "Sometimes (it makes) my tummy hurt."

Nicole: "So it makes you feel uncomfortable, and maybe a little sick?"

Sarah: "Yes."

Joe: "I jump! Like this!"

Nicole: "So you get excited? Or nervous?"

Joe: "I want to hide."

James: "Maybe I can do it, too."

Nicole: "Maybe you can do those bad things, too?"

James: "Yeah."

Nicole: "Do you actually do those bad things, or does it just look and sound like something you could do?"

James: "I cuss."

Sarah: "He does!"

This discussion was held more than one hundred times, and it's representative of the majority of the interactions I had with children. From the range of responses, we can see that some children are disturbed by the violence, some are enervated, and some are inclined to mimic, which is one of the most natural early learning tools. So bad seemed to be a very important behavioral category to include.

Sad

Sad is another major category, and in this context, it means simply anything we see on a screen that makes us feel sad. Discussing screen content that is sad also gives you the opportunity to ask the child whether they feel sad because of what happened in the movie, or if they feel sad because the character feels sad. Right away, this helps the child make a distinction between herself and the character. That's a very important distinction to start making because it opens the door to self-knowing and self-reflection. Also, allowing ourselves to notice and admit sadness felt on behalf of others has a softening effect and opens our hearts to empathy. Knowing what makes your child feel sad is also wonderful information in terms of understanding the child as a person. I'm not suggesting that you try to make children feel sad or that you try to protect them from sadness. I'm saying that being able to notice something sad on a screen, and then notice what you are feeling, has many developmental benefits. We watch screens so much that, if we notice our feelings and reflect on them, the viewing process can help us augment our emotional intelligence instead of numb it.

Scary

The category of scary screen content is the motherlode of diagnostic questions, in part because when you ask a child what they've seen that is scary, you get answers that may shock you. Children tend to have greater retention of details when recalling scary screen moments, possibly because shows, games, and movies that are scary elevate adrenaline. However, the neuroscience behind fear is complex, and the degree of fear certainly impacts remembrance (for example, traumatic fear causes a flood of adrenaline that blurs memory). Still, based on the verbal floodgates that open when children are invited to talk about scary things they've seen on screens, it's safe to say that many children receive a deep impression from frightening screen experiences and often those deeper impressions allow them to retain and verbalize details. Given the fascination our culture has with horror films, we might even term this *recreational fear*. Whether the memories are more powerfully encoded because of adrenaline or the mental pictures are truly more detailed so that children can access them more readily is probably unimportant. Whatever the cause, you will often find that children will be far more verbal and articulate about things that they've seen that are scary.

Combine Gestures with Words to Anchor Vocabulary

When we first introduce fun, bad, sad, and scary (let's abbreviate as FBSS), those words are a pivotal part of the process of starting the dialogue with your child—building trust and opening the door to further disclosures. The deeper use of FBSS to elevate bonding and emotional intelligence is best accompanied by gestures that are repeated by you with the child with a certain amount of energy. It's fun, it's good exercise, and it helps the child remember those categories.

So fun should be said with an upward inflection and raising your arms straight up over your head. Do it again, and then let them do it. Let them lead you, and then do it again.

Now bad. The gesture for bad is facial and physical. You bring your eyebrows down, frown, form two fists and put them on your thighs, and say "Bad." And they might say "Mad," but make sure they're saying "Bad."

For sad, it's very simple. You raise your eyebrows, put your two index fingers right under your eyes and pull down like you're pointing to tears. Use a lighter, more neutral tone rather than trying to sound like you're weeping.

For scary, take those two fists again, raise your shoulders, raise your eyebrows, open your eyes wide and shake a little, saying *"Scaaaary."* You say that with the child.

When they have the physical anchor, the muscle memory, they will better remember the word and they will then be able to start organizing their viewing experiences into those categories. Remember, it's one of the facts of early childhood development that neural networks grow when children are able to create categories for their experiences, and their emotions.[1] By providing children with these simple words, you give them the tools to start sorting the 1,600-hours-a-year mixed bag of viewing experiences into categories. Just that makes the whole FBSS process worthwhile. You're helping your child construct a versatile and satisfying foundation for ongoing discourse and discovery.

> You're helping your child construct a versatile and satisfying foundation for ongoing discourse and discovery.

If your child is extraordinarily precocious and you feel that she or he is much too sophisticated for FBSS, that's fine. Pick another set of words! Better yet, start with FBSS because they'll enjoy participating with you during the physical exercises. Remember, these are word-movement combinations, just like "The Itsy Bitsy Spider," but with a much bigger set of developmental outcomes, including:

❖ Entrée to real dialogue with your children about screen time
❖ Organizing categories to reference and discuss experiences
❖ Stronger recall of categories and experiences that fit those categories
❖ The fun and bonding of shared physical activity

FBSS allows the child to jump-start the process of sorting through past, present, and future media experiences. It is worth its weight in educational gold. After two to three weeks of using FBSS to reference what the child has seen, you'll be able to upgrade the vocabulary very simply by saying, "What's another word besides fun? What are other words that describe something that we like or that we enjoy seeing?" You can see if your child is able to make that step in terms of her vocabulary, or you can start feeding her a few additional vocabulary words by simply using them when prompting your child to talk about something she thought was fun. I'll talk more about expanding the vocabulary for FBSS a little later and show you how to use FBSS for the very first time in Chapter 8.

Prime and Follow Up— FBSS Conversations

What I call the *screen-talk sorting process* of dividing experiences into categories will also start occurring naturally, something that will give you additional traction while talking with children about viewing experiences for which you haven't been present. If, for example, you've okayed viewing a favorite YouTube channel for twenty-five minutes while dinner is being prepared, one of the things you can do with FBSS is to *prime and follow up.*

Before they start watching, you remind them, "So I want you to notice if what you see is fun or bad or sad or scary. And we'll talk about it after dinner." During or after dinner, you get the ball rolling by asking, "So was what you saw fun, bad, sad, or scary? Which ones were fun? Which ones were bad?" That gives you something to talk about over dinner. Again, you're helping the child exercise the process of putting their screen experiences in categories. And this is just the start! A few quick reminders because most of us are pressed for time and these are easy to forget.

1) Delivery and tone of voice matter. It only takes 15 seconds, but you need to sound interested. You're giving the child a "job" and it's a fun job. So you need to keep your voice light and encouraging, raise your eyebrows, smile, and inflect up.

2) Once your child knows the FBSS progression, you can cue it instead of saying the words each time. For example, "While you're watching I want you to notice if what you see is" and then raise your arms up over your head. She'll say, "Fun!" Then you say, "Or" and do the movement for bad. The child will say, "Bad." You say, "Or" and do the movement for scary. After a few times, you don't have to do the movement (unless you want to), you simply pause after the word "is." "I want you to notice if what you watch is . . ." Children can often run through FBSS, cued only by your pause and the word "Or."

  If the child isn't doing the movements, let them know they should do the movements with the words. This gets the heart rate going and the energy up before they start viewing.

3) After three times (or three weeks or three months) you can introduce observations more nuanced than FBSS and prompt higher-order thinking skills. "Tonight when you look for fun or bad or sad or scary, I want you to notice how the program (or movie or game) changes. It can start (do the movement for fun and let the child say fun), but then it can *change*. It could change to show you something (do the gesture for bad and let the child say bad, then do the gesture for sad, etc.). I'll cover this in more depth a little later in the chapter.

After a while, the child himself will get interested in enriching and further specifying these categories. You might be surprised to have your child say, "I don't want to just call it fun, I want to call it things that are funny, things that are pretty, and things that are silly." (And silly isn't always funny; sometimes it's just silly for silly's sake.)

Working with children in all types of schools—affluent, underserved, parochial, and public—taught me to be more specific and consistent in my language when using the FBSS approach. After I had asked children what "scary things" they had seen, James, a three-year-old at Dumas Technology Academy, started talking about seeing a knife. Then he made a stabbing motion in the air and made a motion with two hands if he were opening a lid. He said, "Someone in the garbage." It was clear that James had seen someone stabbed and put into a garbage can or a Dumpster. His fear was palpable and it was affecting the entire class. I had a flash of insight and asked, "Honey, did you see that on a screen or did you see it in real life?" James was so frightened that all he could do was nod when I said, "real life."

At that point, I made eye contact with the whole group and put my hand gently on James's back, saying, "That sounds like it was so scary. I'm so sorry you saw that. But you were really brave to tell us about it. Wasn't he brave?"

The whole class nodded. I asked, "James, would you like a hug?" When James nodded and crawled onto my lap, I said, "Maybe we could all use a little hug. Can you come up one at a time and hug us? You don't have to. Just come on and hug if you want to."

There was a solemn progression of little ones, coming up to James. Some of them put their arms around us, some of them patted his shoulder, some of them just came close and looked at him with tears in their eyes, but all of them cared.

To close the lesson and bring it back to screens, I continued, "What he told us sounds like something no one would ever want to see. Right? But this brave little guy really helped us! Now we know something really important. We *know* we don't like to see things like that in real life. So why would we want to see someone hurt with a knife on a screen?" There was a satisfying chorus of "I don't!"

After that session, I made sure to clarify and ask, "What did you see *on a screen* that was sad?" Even then, some preschool children would start describing something they'd seen in real life that upset them. I never cut them off. If this happens when you're talking with your child, let her elaborate. Even if the session veers a little off course, that's okay. Wouldn't you want to know if your son or daughter saw something really sad they hadn't told you about? Of course you would. Anything that is affecting your child deeply is something you want them to communicate. The process is simple and straightforward, and the more you practice with your little one, the more familiar and comfortable he'll become with your expectation of open communication about screen time.

> Anything that is affecting your child deeply is something you want them to communicate.

When I'm working with very young children in schools, every Screen Smart session starts with questions that invite children to share their viewing experiences over the past week. At the beginning, those experiences are coded and cued with FBSS. So for example, at the end of week one, I'll keep it simple, "Over the next couple of days, when and if you're watching screens, I want you to notice whether what you're watching is fun, bad, sad, or scary. Do you think you can do that?" Giving them an assignment that simply asks them to notice makes the assignment sound like fun, makes it sounds less intimidating, and makes them more likely to do it. You can do that same thing as a parent. It's especially helpful if you know that your child will be with a caregiver over the next couple of days, or someone who is allowing your child to watch more content.

FBSS Applies to Games, Too

I think it's important to note that the terms "fun, bad, sad, and scary" apply to games and apps as much as they apply to narrative content or nonfiction content. If a child is playing a game and you ask them if it was fun, bad, sad, or scary, they can tell you what parts were fun, what parts were bad, what parts were sad, and what parts were scary. By distinguishing those same categories within different types of audiovisual texts and by talking about them, children will gain many of the same cognitive and emotional benefits I've described thus far. With games that involve a lot of violence and aggression, it can be even more important for children to identify FBSS so that they can notice how viewing that content makes them feel.

Building the Benefits of FBSS

There are many benefits to putting FBSS into practice. First, you are giving children categories into which they can begin to sort their experiences and organize them. Second, you're using those words to build a new relationship with your child around and about screens, a relationship that helps them build positive habits of disclosure with a shared set of words. The words themselves are general categories, so the child feels empowered and competent while learning the screen-talk sorting process. Third, the words themselves quickly become springboards for nuanced and complex observation and more sophisticated dialogue.

To build the expanded vocabulary for FBSS, you invite your child to use new and different words in referring to viewing experiences that they've previously called "fun, bad, sad, and scary." But first you can use FBSS to capitalize on the fact that movies, shows, and games are progressive and they change over time as they tell their stories. So at the end of the third or fourth lesson, when we give children a job for the following week, we introduce a new concept that requires additional focus. The job is framed this way: "This week, when and if you watch screens,"—because we never want to tell them they have to or should watch screens—"I want you to notice and tell me how the story in the movie changes. It might start fun and turn into something bad and then become scary, and end with fun. You've seen shows like that, right?"

What you're telling children is that over the course of time, a single audiovisual text can transition among being fun, bad, sad, and scary. But even more advanced is the realization that every moment spent with a screen can be rich and complex. So it could be fun and scary at the same time. It could be fun and a little sad. It could be sad and scary at the same time. It could be bad and scary at the same time.

I usually introduce that idea after six or even ten sessions of co-viewing, and I always use a "roundabout" moment (an emotionally or dramatically complex moment that branches off into many different directions) for that point. For example, when the cuckoo bird tries to fly, I may ask, "How does he feel?" There are numerous correct answers: "Scared. Excited. Worried. Happy." That gives me the chance to observe, "Wow, the bird can feel more than one feeling in the same moment! Let's watch for that in other movies. Let's see if a *story* can be sad and happy and scary at the same time."

You're introducing children to a set of frameworks that will not only allow them to organize their viewing experiences but will allow them to notice the complexity of those experiences from moment-to-moment and the richness and diversity of a specific moment or segment. A media

You're introducing children to a set of frameworks that will not only allow them to organize their viewing experiences but will allow them to notice the complexity of those experiences from moment-to-moment and the richness and diversity of a specific moment or segment.

text can change over time, or it can be very complex and rich in a single moment—those are profound distinctions for a two-, three-, or four-year-old to make consciously. You're teaching the child an appreciation for nuance together with the kind of sustained focus and perceptivity that will allow him to track and notice changes within an audiovisual text. With a very simple base of four words, you're opening the child's awareness to a set of complex observations and insights.

You are also helping children recognize the complexity of emotions within a certain media text as well as within themselves. This has a powerful connection with their social-emotional development. FBSS can easily be used to support social-emotional learning. If you recall, the first distinction in the term "bad" is that screen content can be bad in terms of being poorly produced and uninteresting, or it can be bad in terms of showing actions, events, stories, and information that are not good for us to do, or that makes us feel bad.

Expanding Vocabulary for FBSS

It's best to return to "fun" when you're prompting the child to explore new vocabulary to match their myriad media experiences. I usually say, "Let's start with fun. What are some other words for fun?" Just a few of the vocabulary words that children come up with are entertaining, enjoyable, amusing, pleasurable, uplifting, inspiring, funny, happy, exciting, and silly. Then "bad" quickly translates into rude, mean, violent, naughty, not good, frustrating, boring, ridiculous, awful, dreadful, shocking, terrible, and bossy. Children will come up with many words that are related both to what they're experiencing emotionally and the action that makes them experience it, depending on the action that triggers the emotion.

The same thing will be true of "sad." When a child is two to three years old, it's fine to ask, "Was that a sad TV show?" But as the child becomes more sophisticated and your discussions with her deepen (over weeks, months, or years), you can soothe the concerns instilled by your toughest English teacher by playfully shifting your language at an opportune moment. Jessica, a mother at a school where 90 percent of the children were bilingual, reported that her kindergartener daughter Kiley was repeating FBSS without "going deeper." In a parent-coaching session, I gave Jessica a short script that she used to great advantage. The next time Kiley gave a flat, one-word description of her viewing, Jessica said, smiling, "How can a movie be sad? A movie doesn't have feelings apart from us, does it?" (Then, she waited for Kiley to respond before continuing.) "But a movie can *show us* something sad that might make us feel sad, right? So what did the movie show you that was sad?"

From that point on, Kiley volunteered examples of moments that showed sad things happening, or that made her feel sad.

When you ask your child to share some other words that mean "sad" they may come up with unhappy, whiny, gloomy, miserable, heartbreaking, distressing, disappointing, upsetting, lonely.

Scary is, as I said, the jackpot for responses. Children will say nervous, frightening, terrifying, fidgety, alarming, concerned, intimidating, menacing, spooky, creepy. As we continue to peel back the layers of FBSS and use them in new ways, those words become the keys to opening children's metacognition, their awareness of how they are responding to different experiences. FBSS is a kind of experiential *matrioschka*, the Russian nesting dolls that you keep opening to find others inside. There are many different experiences comprised by those words, and from those experiences children build stronger and more resilient neural networks. You're giving them the tools to create their own refined categories moving forward.

Children won't stay with one-word definitions of their experiences unless you let them. They are constantly changing and learning, so if you simply give them the initial category—like creating a folder for several documents—they will put twenty or thirty experiences in that folder. Then, when you talk with

Prompting children to think of other experiences that they or their friends have had that are similar to what they are seeing on screens is very rich developmentally.

them, they'll start to make text-to-self or text-to-world connections within the contents of that file. Prompting children to think of other experiences that they or their friends have had that are similar to what they are seeing on screens is very rich developmentally. It builds text-to-self connections that boost memory, as well as creates other opportunities to exercise empathy.

Surprising Outcomes

Another surprising outcome from introducing FBSS to young children was reported by teachers during 2011 to 2013, the "proof of concept" years for Screen Smart. At the time, it absolutely stunned me and my researchers.

When I devised the program, I could predict that children's vocabulary, especially the vocabulary related to literacy constructs, would improve. I could predict that their communication skills would improve, and I could predict that there would be an increased number of children who actively participated and communicated during our sessions. I could not predict that tiny children would go home and tell their parents to turn off the TV! It wasn't one of the goals of the program.

Teachers reported that because children had the words fun, bad, sad, and scary, and the ability to distinguish between these categories, they were able to tell their parents what they did and did not want to watch. And they were able to communicate their choices and preferences in ways that adults would hear. Ms. Dee at McCutcheon School said, "Bret told his parents that having the TV on all the time made him feel scared. And he gave examples! So they turned it off." The second year, working with the wise and wonderful Ms. Frankie Betts at Kozminski School, we heard the same exact feedback. Ms. Betts reported that even pre-K students who had always watched "whatever was on" were able to tell their parents, "This is something that is not good for me to watch. This is scary. It will give me nightmares. This is something that I want to turn off."

Simply giving children the words to understand and speak about critical frameworks and categories, followed by practice in expressing their preferences and their observations, made it possible for them to use those skills with their parents. Children felt empowered to tell them what they did not want to watch. Ms. Betts said it best: "These kids have been stuck watching whatever their parents or older siblings are watching. When you teach them these skills, you make it possible for them to be self-determining about their screen choices."

> "These kids have been stuck watching whatever their parents or older siblings are watching. When you teach them these skills, you make it possible for them to be self-determining about their screen choices."

Once children start communicating their experiences to us using FBSS, it gets easier to "prime" viewing experiences and help them use screen time to improve their higher-order thinking skills. Before you turn on or hand a screen to your child, just remind them by saying, "Let's notice what's fun, bad, sad, and scary so we can talk about that." If they miss any categories, then go back and do it again, just make sure that they've had the chance to tell you.

Then within any viewing experience, ask them to notice how the content changes from fun, bad, sad, to scary. That can easily be prompted with the question, "So if we see a movie or play a game, would it be all fun or could parts of it be scary? Or could it be fun, then scary?" Getting them to reflect on the fact that all four of those categories, those characteristics, can be in a single show or movie is an important insight. It gives you the opportunity to point out where and when the content changes. You can ask, "When did the show get scary?" "Did it go back to being fun?" "What happened to make it fun again?" When children have the ability to track those changes, and how movies, shows, and games move back and forth between being fun or showing something bad or showing something scary, it makes them feel in control and augments attention to detail. Later, we'll talk about how tracking those changes gives you the opportunity to talk about how the different "parts" of the movie change to make us feel and notice different things—for example, if the music got loud and scary, if the characters' faces looked different, if the pictures got brighter, or if the setting changed from a cheerful cottage to a dark forest. These types of changes also give you the opportunity to talk about how much fun it is to *notice* changes and keep our minds awake so we can notice what's happening.

Finally, these layers of awareness and learning lead to the ability to discern and notice that screen texts, games, and apps can have many characteristics in the same moment. For example, a scene in a movie or a segment of a game can be scary and sad at the same time. It could be sad and still be enjoyable. Children enjoy learning to make and appreciate those distinctions, and through direct experience they comprehend that, like books, digital content is nuanced and complex and deserving of deeper attention.

Children enjoy learning to make and appreciate those distinctions and through direct experience they comprehend that, like books, digital content is nuanced and complex and deserving of deeper attention.

Chapter 6

Screens Boost Literacy: Plot, Character, Setting, and More

In 2001, right after 9/11, my brother, who was in the Naval Reserves, was mobilized and sent overseas for a year. At the time, my mother took over the care of his two children. Every night after work, I went to help with the dinner, homework, and bed cycle and spent as much time with them as I could on weekends. Between my eight-year-old niece and fourteen-year-old nephew, there was a lot of ferrying back and forth. While I was driving, I would keep them entertained by telling them about some of the films that I was then jurying for the Chicago International Children's Film Festival. Because I saw almost 1,000 movies a year, I had a spectacular array of films with interesting characters and unusual stories to chat about. I apparently shared more than I realized because when I was putting Chloe to bed one night, she popped up with, "Aunt Nicole, tell me another movie," a refrain that was repeated until I got *her* to start telling *me* about the movies and shows she was watching.

Stories Won't Make Sense
Without Structure

For a moment, step outside your educated parent persona and imagine that you are watching a movie for the first time. No one's read you a story yet because you're preverbal so you don't know the words *plot, character,* and *setting.* Suddenly, there's just random but very appealing movement on the screen. There are people and animals and things, but you don't really know what's going on. You may get a sense from the music about who's important, but it's not the same because you can't retrieve that information without the words to describe the image or memories of actions that you can associate with the actions you're seeing on the screen. You can't discuss it. You can't retain new details that are crucial to the development of neural networks without having words to which you can assign all of those qualities of the character. Now you're inhabiting the world of preverbal children.

As the child gets a little older, and has only nascent verbal skills, the process can get more confusing. For example, if you are not aware of plot, then you only know that the images on the screen and the sounds coming from the screen change. And if all change seems to be created equal, no one part is any more important than any other. The absence of identifiers collapses the child's ability to retain, assess, and infer the reasons for each action. If you get to first grade without knowing the definition of plot, and if you don't know that "beginning, middle, and end" and "problem and solution" are *inside* the plot, it takes you a lot longer to practice inferential reasoning with the stories on screens or the stories in books. This

For millions of underserved children, if you can't infer, the achievement gap broadens rather than closes because inference is so crucial to success in academic testing.

simple vocabulary keeps the engine of inference humming along. For millions of underserved children, if you can't infer, the achievement gap broadens rather than closes because inference is so crucial to success in academic testing.

Plot

Part of the success of "telling movies" as stories came naturally from using the same language that teachers use to talk about books in school: character, plot, and setting. Initially, I didn't sit down and teach my niece and nephew those terms, I simply used them. And through the process of inference, they learned very quickly which aspects of the movies were related to character, which were related to plot, and which were related to setting. When they had questions about a part of the movie's story, which they hadn't seen, I would answer their questions using those three key words whenever it was natural. I would also turn their questions back to them (e.g., "Why do *you* think the character said that?"), which not only validated their ideas, but also stimulated their ability to form and voice opinions.

In a nutshell, your children are already smart, and if you use language that allows them to channel and communicate their experiences, you will find out just how smart they are. For example, they have the ability to learn language and structures outside of an active or direct instructional context. You don't have to pretend you're a teacher to familiarize them with narrative structure or vocabulary. Just use the vocabulary when talking with them, and if they don't understand, they will ask you what the words mean. Then you have an opportunity to teach them.

Sometimes a child will ask, "But we're watching a movie, why are you talking about a story?" That's a perfect opportunity to say, "There's a story in a movie, did you know that?" Or ask, "Is there a story in a movie?"

If the child doesn't know or just shrugs, then say, "Well, let's watch for the story and we'll talk about it the way we do when we're reading. At the end of this movie, maybe you can tell me the movie just the way someone would tell me a story. Let's try that!"

Exploring plot during co-viewing or co-playing is especially interesting because story-based films and many games contain a narrative arc that changes over time. They have a beginning, middle, and end, and usually a "problem" or a conflict and a "solution." But when viewing with very young children, it's best to start simply by referencing what happens in the story. "Today, we're going to pay attention to what happens in the story."

When talking about their solo viewing experiences young children often find it easier to describe the action than to answer detailed questions about character and setting. Start generally, "Can you tell me something that happened in the story?" "Can you tell me your favorite part of the story?" After the child answers, if you can get a word in edgewise, you might ask, "Was that from the beginning, the middle, or the end of the story?" You'll notice that when children get the chance to recount "what happened" they sometimes find it hard to stop. No worries! You're exercising their capacity to notice details and describe them, an important twenty-first century skill. As the child answers, you can ask questions for clarification, or to extend the dialogue.

You can even use comments that would technically be considered the wrong answer to affirm the child's observation and redirect it toward the actual question that was asked. So when I ask about the plot (i.e., "What happens in the story?") and a child tells me about the setting, I may smile and say, "What a wonderful answer! But I think you're telling me about the setting, about where the story takes place. I asked you about what happened in the story when . . ." And we go back to our talk.

After we've talked about what happens a couple of times, I'll introduce the word *plot*. "Do you know what the word plot means? Let's say that word—I'll say it, then you say it, then we'll say it together. Plot." (You'll notice the fast interdisciplinary scaffolding here from earlier chapters.) If I think it's a good time to exercise plosives, I may do a 60-second *plosive pop*: a fast exercise of single letters, then a pattern, then a word. It's tempting because children love to make the P sound and the P-T plosive pattern is part of the word plot. Then we'll do a physicalized definition of the word. "Plot is what happens in the story!" And as I say "what happens," I lift my arms up over my head and hold them out like the shape of the letter V. Then I'll return to the screen to continue the program we're watching. If a program or movie is poorly structured or confusing, you can actually deepen the child's understanding of plot by pausing and questioning (or by talking during the program) to ask, "What's happening here?" Or, "What just happened?"

Character

If in co-viewing or co-playing you ask the child to tell you why they enjoy or like a certain character, instead of just saying "So why do you like the bear?" occasionally use the word *character*.

"Why do you like that character?"

And if they say, "Mommy, what's a character?" or "Daddy, what's a character?" then you can say, "Characters are the people, animals, or things in the story or movie." You can also ask, "Do you know what a character is?" If they don't know, give them the simple definition I just used. As I say this sentence, I'll often use a simple rhythmic gesture with my hands to accompany the words I'm speaking. Keeping my hands about ten inches apart with palms flat, I'll do a gentle chopping movement for each word. The movement provides a visual reference and when children do the chopping movement with me, it provides a physical anchor helping them to remember the words.

If I'm working with an older child, I may say, "Characters are the ones that talk and they're the ones that do things in the story. They are the people, animals, or things who move the story forward."

The next time I use the word "character," I may want the child to practice the plosive K sound. "What was the word we learned for the people, the animals, and the things in a story?" If you get no response, give a hint! "It begins with (make the *kuh* sound)." If you still get no response, you can say the whole word character and then have the child say it. "I'll say the word, then you say it. Let's make a big *kuh* sound when we say it." You can even pass the word back and forth like a hot potato, exercising the child's inner mouth muscles with a strong three-syllable pattern.

It's best to start with short media for these purposes, especially short narrative media. Children are very story-oriented, so you're leveraging an existing interest to help them develop an awareness of literacy and narrative structures within that audiovisual text. Using those vocabulary words is also an effective and simple way to get more mileage out of story time. When you are reading stories to children, if you use the word character in relation to characters, you will be giving them a huge head start when it comes to kindergarten readiness. What I'm suggesting that you do with movies and games and television is exactly what you may already be doing with books.

Setting

In schools, when we want to reinforce or introduce the ideas of character, plot, and setting, we start the same way I've advised parents to start—that is, by simply using the terms so that children begin to infer what those terms mean or ask for a definition. I'll ask what the setting is. Then if I'm seeing that they don't understand the word or ask me what setting is, I will redirect the lesson and ask them a question rather than simply providing an answer.

For example, I might say, "There's a special word that means 'where the story takes place.'" When I say, "Where the story takes place," I'll use the rhythmic chopping movement with my hands, just as I did when defining character. Giving children a visual anchor or point of reference with a physical movement will boost retention of the concept.

If we've used the word before, I'll ask, "Does anyone remember that word?"

If we're introducing the word to children ages two to three for the first time, I'll say, "The word for where the story takes place is *setting*. Can you say that word with me?" To cue them, I'll use the little palm "chop" again: "Setting."

As I've said before, if the articulation of the T sound is weak, I'll make a fast game out of pronouncing the T, something I addressed more fully when I talked about plosives. I'll quickly say, "Wait a minute. I don't think I heard the T sound in "seT-Ting." We'll practice the T sound and then say the word *setting* together. Before I go back to the story or the film, I'll repeat: "Setting is where the story takes place." Then, we'll go back to the film, and I'll point to the screen and ask, "What's this setting?"

Often, answers will be very general, so it's fun to get children to be more specific by having them look at the screen for more details. If I've stopped the film on a scene in a living room, children might answer that the setting is a house, or they may answer, "Inside." If they say, "Inside," I'll ask, "Inside what?" Then when they tell me, "Inside a house," I'll say, "Good, inside what room in the house?"

After they've answered what room they think they're seeing, I'll ask them, "Why do you think that's a living room? What kinds of things do we usually see in a living room?" After children get used to the fast rhythm of the questions, they start enjoying answering because they're really good at noticing details. At the end of the film,

I'll often double back and ask, "What's the word we use to describe where the story takes place?"

And they'll tell me "Setting!" Or if they can't I'll make a *sss* sound and give them a hint. Try to avoid just giving a child the answer, even though it's faster and it feels right because you're the parent and an adult. Instead, use their not knowing the answer to ask more questions or give physical or vocal cues that are fun. See how interactive you can make it. You can get them to come halfway. When they're two-thirds of the way, then you can give them the answer with a smile, and have them repeat it.

Then the next time I start co-viewing, I might quickly say, "What is setting?" And once again, I'll make the articulation of that word a game. By making it a game in which a sound is created with strong energy and then repeated with strong energy, they gain a muscle memory—a physical memory of the word. This gives them more than one way to find that information when they're looking for it the next time.

Just remember that the inquiry-based approach to stories, complemented by focus boosters and by rhythmic vocalization and movement, accelerates learning. Sure, you can tell your children "This is character, this is plot, etc." But if you "scaffold" that information with questions, movements, and sounds while co-viewing the film or book, the experience becomes a living laboratory where kids see those words in action and easily identify them. As a bonus, any multisensory approach is going to boost children's focus, engagement, and interest.

Of course, it's hard not to just give children the answers. Most teacher and parent training casts adults as the oracles responsible for unraveling the mysteries of existence for their young charges. Yet there's so much more to be gained from helping the child discover the answer instead of providing it. In a school setting, one of the things I tell all my instructors is, "If you have to *give* a child an answer, you haven't asked the right questions, or layered the interaction with enough clues."

Noticing the Soundtrack

It's probably time to introduce the awareness of another sense that is used constantly in screen time: hearing. Most media will use music to signal and forecast emotions and shifts in dramatic intensity. We want children to be able to notice changes in the music and notice what those changes make them feel and why. Simply pointing out to the child that the music has changed is powerful. The music has changed, they agree. "How has it changed? What does it sound like now?

> We want children to be able to notice changes in the music and notice what those changes make them feel and why.

What did it sound like when the movie started?" "It sounded sad." (Or quiet, etc. The child will give you a lot of different adjectives that tell you what the sound made them feel.)

In the middle of the movie, the music may change to something more upbeat and up-tempo, which suggests to an adult that the character is about to take on a challenge. Children will be able to hear the difference in the music, and the correct question to ask is, "Well, how does that music make us feel now? Because in the beginning, you said that the music made you feel sad!" In the movie *Cuckoo for Two*, the music change signals one of the high points in the dramatic arc— specifically, that the cuckoo bird is about to take a big risk. The tone of the music also suggests that the bird will enjoy taking that risk. So even though the character hesitates, the music is fairly free from fear or concern. Here, I might go back and touch on the plot by saying, "Okay, it's the middle of the movie, the cuckoo bird has been stuck in the clock, and the music is telling us that something has to happen."

Notice that we touched on beginning and middle, now it's the middle, and also we've segued into and added music. Now we're going to ask a higher-level thinking question: "What's the problem?" We start by asking a series of questions that lay the foundation for inference.

Parent: "Where's the green bird? Where's the purple bird? What do they want?"

Child: "They want to be together!"

Parent: "So what's the problem?"

The problem is that they're separated by about eight feet of space. The problem is that they can't reach each other. The problem is that the purple bird is stuck to a perch and the cuckoo bird has never flown before. Children will find one or more of these answers very readily.

"Okay, so now the birds are looking for a solution! Let's see if they find a solution for the problem. Are we ready to watch?"

Sometimes, that far into a film, I'll actually do the priming again. I'll do a quick "shake-stop" (see Chapter 9) or repeat the title of the movie with strong plosives to boost energy. The title of the movie is a lot of fun to say aloud: *Cuckoo for Two.* And it allows you the same kind of playful developmental interaction with your child that unfolds when playing word games or repeating nursery rhymes. You say something and the child repeats it with you. The child says it by himself or herself, and then you say it together. Since *Cuckoo for Two* is fun to say aloud, we'll make the K sound first, three times, then repeat the title, together and individually, before returning to the movie.

The Emotional Pull of Music

Music is the perfect hook to prompt self-awareness, especially the awareness of one's own emotional responses. When a child hears music and starts jumping up and down and dancing, you can ask them (while jumping up and down with them), "How does this music make us feel?" Bear in mind that there isn't a right or wrong answer here.

Music is the perfect hook to prompt self-awareness, especially the awareness of one's own emotional responses.

The question serves the same purpose as a cursor pointing to your interest in the child's experience and response rather than requiring a correct or revealing answer from the child. The child at that point may simply giggle and say, "It makes me feel happy."

"Wow! Music makes us feel happy? Does it make us feel happy all the time?"

"No, sometimes I feel sad when I hear sad music."

Meanwhile you're jumping up and down with your child the whole time. After a couple of questions, stop talking unless the child wants to continue. I'm using this example mostly to show that you can start a dialogue that prompts self-awareness almost anywhere, while doing almost anything. You could easily ask the same questions when playing a game or an app with catchy tunes.

Children can also have different responses to music in different situations and their "music only" responses may be more nuanced than they are when they're watching a character on a screen. In neuro-linguistic programming (NLP), the authors of the system, Richard Bandler and John Grinder, have established three primary prefer-ences.[1] Some of us are primarily auditory, some visual, and some kinesthetic. This doesn't mean that we aren't all auditory, visual, and kinesthetic. It simply means that we have preferred ways in which we respond to and engage stimuli. Many children are visual learners, but they are also very sensitive to auditory stimulation.

I've seen children who cry not because what is happened on the screen is sad, but because the music is making them think of something sad that happened to them. Any powerful and distinctive response is an opportunity for bonding, enriching social and emotional learning (or SEL), and for increasing self-awareness. That's, of course, setting aside extreme responses and adverse reactions, which are not good opportunities for any of those types of interactions.

Reading: A Rainbow of Learning Opportunities

Early childhood training institutions are increasingly focused on teaching educators best practices for leveraging story time so that it becomes an experiential and developmental enrichment process. When you're reading to a child, tone and tempo are as important as when you're speaking to him. I've talked about this in other chapters, but I think it's worth revisiting briefly. If you read too quickly, you know that the child will get impatient and/or confused, losing track of the story. If you use a monotone, the child will lose interest. But most important, if you don't allow time for interaction, you're missing 50 percent of the growth potential that reading aloud to your child offers.

That growth potential comes from understanding that story time (or even app time) creates an authentic parent-child sphere of interaction. It's a magical bubble in which questions can be asked, appreciation of illustrations and events can be shared, plus there's room for a whole lot of giggling and cuddling. Reading together is a winning trifecta of auditory, visual, and kinesthetic stimulation that strengthens

Reading together is a winning trifecta of auditory, visual, and kinesthetic stimulation that strengthens the parent-child bond while also providing vast opportunities for developing new neural networks.

the parent-child bond while also providing vast opportunities for developing new neural networks.

In any picture book, you have the opportunity to count characters or objects on a page so you can suddenly segue into a math opportunity. You also have the chance to identify the colors, and very young children need that kind of practice. They need experiences in which the identification of any category or new word happens during an engaging activity instead of as a result of abstract instruction.

I've walked into many classrooms where a teacher holds up a flash card or points to a color on a Promethean board (an interactive whiteboard) and says, "Here is the color yellow. Let's say *yellow*."

That's not nearly as much fun as looking at a picture where a vibrant sun is rising over a garden, pointing to it, and asking, "What is that color?"

Then, "What is the shape?"

"What do we think it is? If it comes up in the morning, what could it be?"

If the answer isn't coming, I might give a hint, "The *ssssu . . .*"

"The sun!"

"Yes, it's the sun. What color is the sun? In this book, what is the color of the sun?"

You've spoken forty or fifty words back and forth. These words are inestimably precious and valuable in early childhood. While reading books aloud may be the go-to activity for vocabulary-building according to psychologist Dominic Massaro, talking with them builds communication skills and confidence.[2] You're strengthening developmental domains every time you reach into the reading experience and ask questions that let the child demonstrate how well they've grasped even the most (to you) basic concepts. Everything is new for them. If they can answer simple questions and own the answers, you are giving them a more lasting, enduring educational experience than they would normally have from a quick "read through." It's also a way to acclimate your child to the Socratic learning process, which is the richest and fullest learning modality, offering the best learning outcomes long-term for most children.

A quick thought: with very young children, it's wise not to have the expectation of linear progress in learning. That means even if your three-year-old seems to grasp and understand the word *character,* two nights before, he might forget it by the third night or he might be too tired. He may simply not want to hear that word. You have to be flexible in the way you interact with the child, but that flexibility doesn't mean talking down to them or babying them or using the high-pitched voice that infantilizes most children. Instead, it's wise to notice or prompt and stimulate them to find out what interests them most that day.

Expand the Toolbox of Words

Another way that knowing character, plot, and setting strengthens children's higher-order thinking and grasp of narrative structures is that it gives them additional categories into which they can organize their viewing experiences. As I've said before, children benefit enormously from learning and applying new words that allow them to sort their experiences into categories. All experiences become valuable when they can be sorted into categories. Think of those categories as the tables in an interrelational database. Layer by layer, word by word, experience by experience children are building their own interrelational databases. From the simplest categories, children's brains build neural networks that can interface and lead to higher-order thinking.

The classic who, what, when, where, why journalistic words are also helpful when framing questions in ways that help very young children get comfortable with critical thinking about character, plot, and setting. Here's a simple rule:

Who = character
What = story or details
Where/When = setting
Why = critical thinking

You start with the easiest words, prompting with questions and suggestions such as:

"Let's notice *who* has the most fun during the program."
"We're going to talk about *where* we saw things happening."
"Can you tell me *what* happened at the beginning?"

As the child gets older and you introduce plot, character, and setting, you can tie the words they've heard and used for the past year into the simple definitions. The who-what-when-where-why approach is a hit with children and another brick in the road toward kindergarten readiness.

Here's a quick example of what building your child's interrelational story database looks like, starting with the categories we create first—fun, bad, sad, scary. Within FBSS, there are at least eight to ten subcategories and definitions for each word. So FBSS generates a good-sized initial web into which children can generally sort their viewing experiences. But moving forward, you add additional organizing principles: plot, character, setting; whether I like it or do not like it and why; what I feel and think about plot, character, setting, etc. Those structures and principles continue to get more sophisticated and complex as children continue viewing.

Children realize that over the course of a plot, their feelings about these specifics may change. Characters, settings, and plot may also change over time in the story, and within those structures, the child develops a deepening awareness of specifics and details that allow him to form increasingly refined and defined opinions and ideas.

That's how you (and your children) get to higher-order thinking. You start from the most general, universal categories, and then enrich and enhance them through new experiences, reflection, assessment, communication, and understanding of each of those categories. As you accumulate more viewing and reading experiences with the active, intentional use of these words and questions, the child will build wonderfully complex and flexible neural networks capable of processing, perceiving, and expressing increasingly sophisticated ideas. The ability to infer and think with depth and subtlety evolves naturally, layer by layer, during viewing, noticing, discussion, questioning, answering, and feeling.

Review of Steps to Amplify Neural Networks

1) Start with the simplest words that allow children to start organizing their experiences.

2) Prompt or allow the child to come up with additional words (homonyms, synonyms, refinements) because you want to offer the child new stimulation. As you continue talking, you'll notice when FBSS becomes too easy because the answers will appear automatic.

3) Introduce the words *character, plot,* and *setting, beginning, middle,* and *end,* and *problem* and *solution* to help the child form the fundamental neural networks that allow them to formulate new ideas and responses to what they've seen or read.

Chapter 7

Our Values, Our Screens

In today's divisive world, tackling a word like *values* can make us uncomfortable so I want to be clear about what I mean. Values don't label or pigeonhole you as having a specific religious orientation. Very young children learn values and character from parental actions and attitudes just the way a sponge absorbs water. Kindness, caring, compassion, generosity, dignity, self-respect, and respect for others are values that children will learn from watching you. Those values aren't limited to a single religion or philosophy. In fact, it's hard to envision sharing a civilization without those values because they're part of a fundamental human social contract. They make it possible for us to honor diversity and share this planet in rewarding and meaningful

Very young children learn values and character from parental actions and attitudes just the way a sponge absorbs water. Kindness, caring, compassion, generosity, dignity, self-respect, and respect for others are values that children will learn from watching you.

ways. But we've run into a problem because that social contract has been broken—some would say shattered—not just by actions, but by the quality of discourse, the fracturing and manipulation of words and images on screens.

If very young children continue spending 1,600 hours a year watching screens, it's even more essential that you, the parent, become a trusted mentor who can interact with your child during screen time. Instead of being merely a media protector who confines children to limited screen choices, you can be a guide to help your child navigate powerful screen influences, and discover whether the values your child is absorbing are really the values that you're trying to impart.

I know you're trying to impart values. I know you're saying "Share" and "Don't hit" and "Let's keep our voices down" when you go into a public space. I know you're trying to give your child the right foundations for interacting with others in society. But if your son or daughter often sees images on screens that contradict your instructions for good behavior without a trusted adult mediating those images, your child will naturally be confused.

Think about it. I'm two years old. Here's what Mommy tells me to do. Here's what I see on my tablet. We're asking children to navigate a moral abyss that can't be crossed by most adults, let alone a two-year-old. And in the absence of interaction with a caring adult, the positive traits and behaviors you're trying to help him cultivate will be slowly but surely eroded. It can be very simple to intervene while watching the kind of random, offhand cruelty you see in many popular movies and television shows, even on approved "kids' networks." Without lecturing or yelling, you can say "Hey, wait a minute, what's wrong with this picture? Last night we just agreed on something. We said we're not going to make fun of our little brother, right? Why? Because it's making him feel bad. So did you notice what just happened on the screen? Is that something we're going to do in our own family?"

Teaching a child to become Screen Smart can deepen and rein-force family values. Rather than panicking when they discover that their children have viewed "inappropriate" narrative content, par-ents can use those experiences to enrich a child's ability to discern basic ethical and moral questions. You'll learn how to teach a child how to process content from a value-centric perspective. This chap-ter provides a fresh, new way to approach the question: Is what my child watching enhancing or eroding what I believe in? I'll also offer suggestions and strategies for how talking about screen content can help get things back on track for the entire family. We'll chal-lenge current dogma about what's appropriate and not appropriate for children to watch on screens, how those questions should be reframed, and why.

We have to approach the issues of the quality or appropriateness of content from a completely new perspective. Concern about con-tent isn't limited to what we find in discrete programs, movies, or commercial. It extends to memes, news items, and even Internet ads because once a child gets online, the organization of content, as well as its design, headline, and photo illustration constitute another kind of messaging. For example, on AOL or Yahoo News online, a fasci-nating academic study on bullying may be positioned next to Nicki Minaj's bare breasts at fashion week. The seemingly random juxtapo-sition is actually a deliberate ploy to attract "eyeballs" (i.e., attention) but in a child's mind such positioning can create confusion, false equivalence, and normative expectations that nudity and salacious content are culturally acceptable.

In the crazy-quilt world of digital news, there are myriad issues of appropriateness with regard to the behavior of political figures, celeb-rities, police, medical, or financial professionals—the list is endless. Anyone on the planet in range of a phone camera is subject to being sliced and diced for Internet scrutiny.

> When it comes to Internet, film, social media, or games, your own family and community choose, clarify, and constitute their specific definitions of appropriateness.

When it comes to Internet, film, social media, or games, your own family and community choose, clarify, and constitute their specific definitions of appropriateness. This means that whatever is acceptable for your family's cultural, spiritual, or developmental values would be appropriate. While I vote for being selective and limiting my news feeds and access, you may be a news (or celebrity, or fashion, or Comic-Con) omnivore. For children, I think that author Lisa Guernsey's guidelines are germane and useful. She advises adults to consider the context in which the media is being used and the aptitude, temperament, limitations, and strengths of your own child to determine the appropriateness of fiction, nonfiction, and advertising content.[1] But if you're *starting* your screen-time odyssey by trying to judge the appropriateness of content, it's going to be bewildering because there is so much content, there are so many different kinds of content, and there are so many different places where your child is going to be exposed to it. Common Sense Media provides one of the most comprehensive, age-appropriate guides for selecting various types of media and games. You're not alone in the search for appropriate content and www.commonsense.org is a good friend for parents.

So instead of starting from that perspective, why not start by setting up the best possible lines of communication between you and your child? Then broaden that communication to the whole family, so that you establish a family culture that includes and supports talking and conversation.

Creating a New Family Culture Around Digital Devices

A positive family culture starts by building good relationships and good communication. When it comes to digital devices, you need to develop one-on-one relationships where children want to share their experiences and come to you with their questions. The child then knows that talking with family members about their digital experiences is enjoyable, and that their views are valued.

For whole-family communication, it's helpful to create a family agreement for discussions. Print it out and share it with your children, letting them give some input. One-on-one with a two-year-old, that agreement is implicit and very simple. When you talk, I listen; when I talk, you listen. No yelling, hitting, or crying. But for families with children at different ages, it's great to have a family agreement that supports real discussion. For example:

One diva, one mike. When we talk, one person talks at a time.
We use indoor voices.
We don't attack one another's ideas or accuse.
We ask questions and listen to answers.

Type it up in an interesting font, make it colorful, and you've got something you can keep on the fridge or in the family room! Even if you only hold one family meeting a year, having a family agreement about discussions helps stabilize your family culture and transmit its values. The caring, inclusive characteristics of the discussion come through loud and clear to children. You're showing that you care about what they say, the way they say it, and how they're heard by the whole family. The agreement supports the value of each family member in the discussion.

When you give children
direct experience with
collaborative communica-
tion, you're giving them a
powerful foundation for
social engagement.

When you give children direct experience with collaborative communication,
you're giving them a powerful foundation
for social engagement. They'll be able to
integrate themselves into many other
types of discussions with equanimity
and confidence. You're also giving them
an experience with positive group discourse that will shrink the incli-
nation to bully. They'll have seen and felt the value of each person's
contribution, and they'll have had experience controlling their own
"attack" impulses. Those are really powerful tools.

To summarize, instead of just approaching screen choices from
the perspective of what's appropriate, let's use screen talk to build the
kind of relationship with our children that allows them to freely bring
us their feelings and questions. Let's keep the door to the parent as
a mentor and guide fully open. Let's create supportive frameworks
for individual and family discussion. Finally, let's help children to
develop the filters that will allow *them* to identify what they feel is
good for them, what they enjoy, what they want to experience more
of, and what they think is disturbing, not good for them, and don't
want to see.

Remember, we begin by opening the child's mind to notice and
share his or her own perceptions from the very beginning of their
experiences with screens. This is the first step in setting up the loom
to create their own filters. The warp is what I like, what I don't like
and why, how what I see makes me feel, and what it makes me think.
The weft is FBSS and plot, character, setting. To these, children will
add color and nuance and thousands of threads. They'll be able to
track their own growth by virtue of the fact that they'll keep noticing
details, then sharing and talking with you, their friends, and teachers
about what they've noticed. And you, the parent, will keep guiding

them to keep those threads straight. If the threads get tangled, they'll come to you, and you'll help them untangle the warp and weft of the filters that they're weaving for their screen-time experiences. It's all predicated on creating interactive relationships and communication around digital devices. If children form a one-way relationship with screens, everything goes into their brains and becomes a roiling, uncomfortable mass of electronic content constantly stimulating the right side of the brain and the lower so-called "reptilian" brainstem. You already know how too many hours of viewing affect your otherwise able-bodied child. But more important, she should know and notice how "too much screen time" makes her feel. Then the motivation to cut back will come from her, rather than simply being enforced by you. Naturally, in the twenty-first century when many homes contain screens numbering in the double digits, you'll need "the basics" for keeping digital devices in their place.

> **What they watch or use**—Select appropriate content and devices and apps. Balance the context of viewing with the temperament of your child and use the many fine, mostly free online resources to aid in selection. Some even connect to reading or guide you through ways to talk to children about commercials.
> **When they watch or use**—Create a daily and weekly schedule. For older children screen time should come after chores and homework. For very young children, allocate screen time throughout the day when it's most beneficial and convenient.
> **How much they watch or use**—Although I've said this is a personal choice, the American Academy of Pediatrics has good guidelines and good reasons for those guidelines. Children ages eighteen months and under can't understand screen content and using the screen as a pacifier has known downsides, including temper tantrums when screens aren't available and

early formation of addiction. If you can't talk to them about their feelings and thoughts, I'd limit screen time to less than an hour, if that. If your child is verbal, stick to a sixty- to ninety-minute limit and monitor how she responds. If you sail into a really rocky harbor and you notice that your young child loses sleep, focus, and mental acuity, just pull back and turn it all off.

In 2018, the World Health Organization officially named *gaming disorder* to its disease list. Being hooked on gaming is especially dangerous for the youngest gamers with developing brains. There's plenty of research that shows how gaming can take over a child's life. (It's important to remember that addiction is not defined by substance, but by compulsion.)

According to Victoria L. Dunckley, MD, vast numbers of children now suffer from electronic screen syndrome (ESS), a "disorder of dysregulation" defined as "the inability to modulate one's mood, attention level or arousal in a manner appropriate to one's environment." Dunckley's book, *Reset Your Child's Brain* offers valuable insights into media "fasting."[2]

Sandra Bond Chapman, author of *Make Your Brain Smarter* and the director of the Center for Brain Health at the University of Texas at Dallas, addresses parental concerns about children's dependence on digital devices with the recommendation that they "embrace the technology not punish them with it."[3] For teens Chapman recommends what she calls *interval training*. Kids spend thirty minutes doing homework without any disruption from technology, then during the next half hour of homework, they can check their phones or other devices. Chapman says that teens who do the experiment are amazed by how much less time it takes them to do homework and how much better they retain information when they're not distracted by digital devices.

"Wise Blood"

In 2006, I was seeking support for MediaBridge, a program that would bring young people together from all over the world for an intensive workshop similar to the Sundance Screenwriters Lab, but for high-school aged youth. While pitching the program to different funders, one prospective grantor shared her own fascinating story. The super-bright VP of the foundation told me that one of the most terrifying and impactful experiences she had as a child was seeing the film *Wise Blood* with her parents at age ten. Based on Flannery O'Connor's 1952 novel, the film was directed by John Huston in 1979 and is a wrenching parable about the challenges to faith and redemption in the modern world. Given the disturbing content, one could easily argue that this was not an appropriate film for a ten-year-old to view. At the same time, what rescued that experience was the enviable trust and confidence that the girl's parents had instilled in their daughter from the time she was very young. She was supported by the understanding that her "ideas contributed to the culture of the family." Almost anything she said would be welcomed and not judged. Her questions would be answered and if the answers were unsatisfying, she was allowed to probe more deeply. She described a fascinating process, one that moved from discussion to reflection to observation, then back to reflection and discussion over the course of months. Initially, talking with her parents, she had access to their insights and ideas about the film, while feeling free to express her own honest feelings of being disturbed. Knowing that she could keep referencing and talking about her feelings, she independently started making (text-to-world) connections between scenes she had seen in the film and the experiences of Holocaust survivors at her synagogue, and volatile behaviors by children at her school. This melting pot of impressions, images, and feelings were sorted and processed over time because she was able to share her observations and emotions and ask her parents about each of those experiences. However, the outcome might have been very different in the absence of such an emotionally and intellectually supportive environment, or with a more nervous or sensitive child.

Here's an observation you may find surprising. On a one-time or seldom basis, most children really won't be "damaged" by viewing inappropriate screen content. They are especially resilient if (a) they've had some positive priming before viewing; (b) they know they can come to you and talk about their experiences during or after viewing; and, (c) they're not watching it all the time.

> It's important to respect your child's limits and preferences, so forcing or imposing a viewing experience on your child is never a good idea.

That said, it's important to respect your child's limits and preferences, so forcing or imposing a viewing experience on your child is never a good idea. But if she happens to see something truly disturbing on your watch, having the open door to dialogue will be a lifesaver. You can have the confidence of knowing that if she does come to you quivering with fear, you can effectively support your child with this framework of inquiry, care, and interest. The underlying message is, "Whatever you want to talk about, I want to hear, and if you just want to cuddle, that's fine, too."

Provided you're not panicking or projecting on your child after discovering she's seen abominable content, she'll be fine. When your child does see something that one would say isn't beneficial for them, the first step is to stay calm. Then, if the child is willing to talk, you can start a great dialogue with questions that derive from your understanding of the child and what they've seen. If they've seen a horror film or horrific news of some kind: "What part was upsetting? What did you notice about that?" If you can get them into logic and objective assessment, it's going to slow down the emotional hamster wheel that they're running on. Just remember: the tone needs to be open and positive and supportive and interested. You can gently explore what they're feeling now, why they're feeling that, and what would feel best right now. Would a quick look at the tricks of movie-making help, or would lap time and a gentle, "I'm so sorry you saw that" be a bigger comfort? Does the child want to draw a picture of what he saw and rip it up? When the emotions are winding down, it's helpful and reassuring to affirm that the child never has to experience that kind of movie or game or program again. Now that he knows how upsetting it can be, he can make good choices. Then you can move on to "Let's do something fun and get your mind off it!" That can be a perfectly acceptable way of helping to redirect "the upset."

If the child still has things that he wants to bring up, go for it as long as the emotions continue to stabilize. Just know that it is extremely unlikely that there would be any form of lasting damage, especially if you swiftly engage your child when he or she will be most receptive and responsive to your support.

Discipline Versus Dialogue

The temptation to continue to build safe media bubbles for our children is there, and we understand why. Between easily accessed pornography and truly vile videos on YouTube, there certainly appears to be a proliferation of content that seems to be dangerous and harmful. At the same time, we need to stay the course with respect to focusing on what we *do* want for our children, rather than what we *don't* want. If we focus on what we don't want, our apprehensiveness will be communicated to our children, often prompting them to see those unwanted by parent screen experiences as more attractive. They will seem like forbidden fruit.

By focusing instead on *the relationship I want my child to have with screens*, we can appreciate the positive things and build on strengths. We'll see how they can build their own filters and start to notice how screen time is making them feel. They will start to make decisions based on honest, aware assessments of how they are responding to digital content. You end up being the joyful recipient of your child's perceptions and shared experiences. When the door to dialogue is open, you won't have the same disciplinary issues around screen time because the dynamic will shift.

Of course, that only happens after your child is acclimated to talking with you! Once you've gotten the process of priming down, and the child is enjoying the process of sharing her digital odysseys, you're operating in a twenty-first century family paradigm. Instead of being segregated, screen experiences are part of the sphere of family and parent-child communication.

Here's an outcome that might surprise you in a few years when you've been using Screen Smart skills with your children. If you're worried about something your older child might see, there's a good chance she'll talk to *you* about it. Let her ask you if she can watch something! That discussion goes something like this:

Child: "I really want to see *Game of Thrones* once. All my friends watch it."

Adult: "I don't want you watching *Game of Thrones*. You're only eight years old."

Child: "Could you let me watch it once and then we can talk about it? Maybe you could watch it with me and answer my questions?"

This is a dialogue that demonstrates a strong bond of trust and respect. It validates the child as an individual and supports her curiosity while confirming your role as mentor and guide. You're creating community and closeness around screens and interacting with electronic devices in new ways. Now, regulating screen time isn't about discipline, it's about creating navigation buoys.

Content That May Be Contrary to Your Family Values

A great example of using family navigation buoys was reported by a good friend and validated by his children after he attended one of my workshops. Rick told me that he had picked *Home Alone* for a family movie night film. In the first ten minutes of the screening, Rick said he got up, stopped it, turned to the kids (who were ages six to thirteen) and actually said, "Okay, what's wrong with this picture?"

Right away, the eldest boy responded, "The parents are allowing all the older kids to be really mean to the youngest kid. It's kind of the opposite of what you've told us to do."

The middle boy asked Rick why the filmmaker would do that. Rick, who is gifted in asking open-ended questions, turned the question back to the boys and said, "Why do you think he would show the parents allowing the older children to be so cruel to the youngest child?"

And the oldest boy said, "Well, it kind of fits the narrative of the kid needing and wanting to get away from everybody."

Then the youngest boy said, "That's not the way anyone in a family should treat anyone else. Maybe we shouldn't bother watching this because if it starts with that, there's no chance it's going to get better."

When you run up against content that's inappropriate for your family, it's a great idea to notice that. Saying, "Wait a minute, this is off-base," then talking about it and making a

> When you run up against content that's inappropriate for your family, it's a great idea to notice that. Saying, "Wait a minute, this is off-base," then talking about it and making a decision together strengthens everything you're teaching your children.

decision together strengthens everything you're teaching your children. Rick's family *could have* watched more and talked more but in that case, everyone just decided not to watch the film. It's a great example of the way the moral abyss that looms every time we turn on television can be crossed with constructive dialogue. However, that abyss can't be bridged as reliably by the didactic approach or lectures and explanations.

Let's briefly revisit normative impressions that kids get from digital devices. There is a lot of content that seems benign in comparison to content about sex, drugs, and violence. But when very young children *repeatedly* view casual rudeness, abrasive behavior, or "mild" dishonesty, just remember you're inviting those behaviors into your family. Many people can recognize this, and yet they somehow think their own families are exempt.

An article in the entertainment trade magazine *Variety* presented some fascinating statistics in 2004. The article gave a profile on young men who were writing television shows for children ages eight to thirteen, calculated how often children were depicted in mainstream media, and discussed what some of the writers' biases appeared to be. The first statistic was that children are conspicuously absent from 80 percent of film and television content. (Okay, that's changed with YouTube but there are as many kittens and puppies as kids.) For the 20 percent of the time that children are included, they are shown having *no* responsibilities in the home 90 percent of the time. Now think for a moment. How many times in real life have you seen a child's room looking like a tornado hit it, with parents helplessly complaining about that fact?

This so-called "benign" messaging can be incredibly destructive to families. Countless parents have told me that their children resist doing chores saying, "None of my friends have to do them." But they're not talking about their real friends; they're talking about their electronic peers! When they say that "Everyone else's room looks like mine," they're talking about rooms they've seen on digital devices. Accepting this kind of behavior as normative without discussion makes children feel like they don't need to contribute to their families, and that they should have no responsibilities. As these feelings become entrenched, children often become increasingly resentful of anything they're asked to do. If they start watching kids-have-no-chores content when they're tiny and have older brothers and sisters who always cover their responsibilities, some of the most entrenched resistance to chores can come from your youngest children.

Of course, there are always exceptions, and your child may be a natural "helper" like little Louis Conant, the brother of a student of mine. Louis was an eight-year-old with a big heart who carried the tray of a kindergartener at lunch every day because he "worried about her."

But look down the road at the "no chores" kids. Slacker and slob stereotypes aside, it's depressing to live in a room that smells like an old sock. It's demoralizing when you never have any clean clothes and don't know how to take care of yourself because someone else has always taken care of those everyday details. You can argue that this is only the case in affluent families where parents "took over" kids' lives, but you'd be wrong. It happens to children in families of all economic levels.

So who was writing the shows that preempted parenting manuals? According to *Variety,* the majority were white males ages twenty-four to twenty-five who didn't like having responsibilities themselves and thought it was hilarious if a five-year-old used the F-word. Yikes! Were we really allowing our culture to be influenced by the childhood resentments of random guys writing kids' sitcoms?

I have a Taiwanese friend in his late seventies who took the family water buffalo to their rice fields every day, starting when he was six-years-old. When I was nine, my mother trusted me to take my baby brother to the park when he was less than a year old. I can give you scores of other examples of elevated levels of responsibility that gave children tremendous confidence and belief in their own abilities. Please don't think I'm advocating for childhood-crushing levels of responsibilities—I'm not. I'm just wondering if we can't do better than allowing our children's imaginations to be driven by people who find it expedient to lash out at their own childhoods through the medium of their "art."

The good news is that some content creators *are* doing better. The majority of successful pre-K shows now have early childhood experts who work with their writing teams, and that model has caught on as the importance of character building gained traction. As I've said, Common Sense Media offers some excellent resources for helping parents select programs. But take a quick look at these shows yourself from time to time. And if you see the stereotypes of the "stupid parents" of "clever kids with messy rooms," just use it as an excuse to start a great conversation with your kids.

When You Feel Like You Might Stop Caring

Adults often tell me they're concerned that their own values are being affected by the avalanche of violence, sexual content, cruelty, and crassness. "It's like an anesthetic—I'm worried that I'm going to stop caring," said one Gen Y mom. The technique we use with festival juries and selection committees of all ages can be helpful here. To select the best content, they need to keep criteria in their minds while viewing. So just work out what you want to watch for, write it down, and make that your own criteria. While viewing, you may want to glance at it one or two times so it stays fresh. After a few days, you'll develop a clear sense of what you should or shouldn't be watching and you'll start to feel empowered to make your own viewing changes.

Here's what a list of criteria might look like:

My Criteria

What I Want from Viewing

- ✓ To laugh
- ✓ To feel entertained
- ✓ To be soothed and calmed
- ✓ To learn something I never knew before
- ✓ To be inspired to act in new ways

What I Don't Want

- ✓ Random, gratuitous violence
- ✓ Random, gratuitous sex and nudity
- ✓ Random profanity
- ✓ Lack of consequences for violent/selfish/criminal behavior
- ✓ Glamorization of unsavory characters aka "glitter on a pig"
- ✓ To feel that life is dark and danger is inescapable
- ✓ To feel anxious

After twelve sessions of Screen Smart at Darwin School, first-grade teacher Ms. Bidne said, "Noticing how something makes you feel helps you change. I turned on *Criminal Minds* two days ago and after about ten minutes I turned it off. I noticed it was making me feel queasy and uncomfortable. But before this, I would have just sat and watched anyway. It made a big difference in my sleep. I'm going to be way more picky in the future."

Values-Centric Viewing

There's an easy way to strengthen a child's ability to notice conflicts between your values and screen content. Just ask her to keep a specific value in mind while viewing. The next time she watches something, ask her to notice a different value. As a parent or caregiver, you do it when you prime before viewing. Noticing is part of the fun of co-viewing or solo viewing.

Then, after you've encouraged the child to use energy/concentration and keep her mind awake, you add a values-related "job":

Today let's notice if any of the characters help one another in the movie.

Today let's notice if any of the characters are being selfish.

Today let's notice if someone says something when a character is naughty.

Today let's notice how it makes us feel if someone is kind to someone else in the show.

Today let's notice how the brothers and sisters treat each other.

Movies, Commercials, and Games, Oh My!

Screen Smart skills and screen talk are invaluable for defusing upsetting behaviors in young children, especially if those skills are in place before they've seen something violent, cruel, or supremely persuasive. Think about what happens if you're teaching your child to share, be nice, and care about others, and he happens to play GTA III (Grand Theft Auto III) with his friend's older sibling, see a commercial for a cool robot, or accidentally wander into a movie where characters are fighting and screaming.

At a recent parent workshop, one young father said, "Telling my four-year-old son 'Calm down, it's just a movie' didn't work. He started kicking and hitting his seat along with the movie. It was like watching with him gave him permission to act out the way the characters did. So we left the theater and had a talk instead." Good call.

You're going to want to address contradictions between what you're saying as a parent and what the characters are doing onscreen. Otherwise your presence during co-viewing can confer tacit parental permission to act out the way the characters are acting in the movie. If we don't want time spent with digital devices to foster disruptive and undesirable behaviors, then we need to talk about what they've seen and how they're responding to it. That's true whether the child is gaming, playing with apps, watching YouTube, movies, or the news.

The basic principles of the Screen Smart approach apply no matter the device, content, or technology. Here, I'm going to outline a simple technique that I've used many times. It's helpful when children come to me upset about things they've seen, or when parents have begged for "something to say" after forgetting to prime the child's mind and then finding the child glued to something salacious or violent. We call it "rebooting the brain and using details to redirect."

If the child comes to you, don't just start talking directly about a school shooting, a Cialis commercial, or the sex scene that's just flashed by on a YouTube Kids video. Mentally hit the reset button and start with:

"Wait, were you using your energy and concentration? Let's get some energy going." Take a second to do the shake/stop and ask, "Is your mind awake? What questions would you like to ask me?"

In some cases, the child may express a feeling, often concern or fear; in others he may let loose a flurry of disorganized words. Your job is to guide his attention to specifics, letting his observations provide structure and order so that you can provide context and help him find meaning.

"What did you see on the screen when you got upset?"

"Shooting. Fall down."

"Was it outside or inside?"

"Outside."

"Was it nighttime or daytime?

"Day time. And see police."

Do you see where we're going here? By the time the child has recounted the details, he'll feel calmer, less concerned, and more in control.

"Wow, you really noticed a lot! I'm proud of you." This would be a good moment for a hug. At that point, fully 50 percent of the time, the child will go back to playing, or ask for a treat. If the child continues, keep listening.

"Someone hurt."

"I'm so sorry you saw that. I know we don't like it when people get hurt. Maybe you can send a kiss or a smile. Make that person feel better." If your family prays together this is a wonderful moment to say, "Let's say a little prayer for that person."

If you're the one who notices a problematic behavior onscreen or notices problematic behavior in response to the screen, stopping to talk is your first step.

Just let the child know, without blame, "Hey, this isn't the way we act. Let's pause and talk a little." Then deflect and redirect the issue by asking questions about the characters, the effects, what the child noticed, etc. You'll get him back on track behaviorally, find common ground, and *then* you can ask a sincere question like, "Are those the kinds of things we want to do (at home, in a theater, to our friends, etc.)?" Let the child say "no" and then continue. "So that's why we're going to stop watching (playing) that movie (or game) right now." Note that you're not using the word *never*. "I'll never let you watch that" is a needless red flag for a child, but, as a parent, you know that "right now" can last a long time.

Is Childhood
Oversexualized by Screens?

As a culture and as adults who care about kids, we need to face the fact that children are being marinated in sexual content from the time they're tiny. Movies, television, games, magazines, billboards, and cross-platform advertising are highly sexualized, objectifying men and women, boys and girls. As the boundaries of what's culturally acceptable roll back further and further, the opportunities for your child to be exposed to sexualized messages proliferate. Children may not fully understand those images, but that doesn't mean they're not affected by them, nor does it mean they're not absorbing the underlying messages of those meanings. Our youngest children learn through imitation. If they constantly see adults on screens embracing and using the terms "hot" and "sexy," they're going to try them out, too. Every year for the past seven years, early childhood teachers have reported to me that five- and six-year-old boys "tell girls they are 'sexy,' without even knowing what that means," and girls as young as pre-K tell other children that it's "good to look hot." Flash forward six years to sixth, seventh, or eighth grade. How can we blame our children for providing oral sex services to one another if they are acclimated to expect those images as a "normal" part of twenty-first century screen time? You can rationalize it as a 200-year-old pendulum swinging back from our Puritan roots, but if you check your inner moral compass, you'll know it's not healthy.

Of course, I don't have a problem with children being exposed to sexualized content when they've been prepared for it, and are capable of understanding it and noticing its effect on them. But we should all have a huge problem with children being exposed to "sex that sells" everything from cars to cabinets. Those images make children feel that "This is what everybody does" before they understand what sex *is.* It's extraordinarily damaging because larger and larger numbers of young children will simply incline toward experiences that they are not sociologically, psychologically, or emotionally equipped to deal with. You may have managed to block out the digital sexual imagery that populates your devices, but your children haven't.

After the R-rated movie *Thirteen* came out in 2003, about a teenage girl who falls into a dangerous friendship with a troubled teen, Oprah had an interesting show where she invited mothers to do an exercise in co-viewing. She asked them to sit with their young children and watch a show they thought was acceptable or benign. Their job was simply to make a hatch mark every time they saw a sexual incident or heard a sexual joke or reference. To their great credit, many of these moms were genuinely embarrassed; they blushed on national television while confessing to having seen "far more sexual content" than they expected on the shows they thought were "fine." As I recall, *Friends*, which is still broadly syndicated, was one of the programs shown widely during "family prime time" between 5 and 6 PM in the 2000s. (For several years, so was *Family Guy*, a network choice that was patently bewildering unless the programmer had never seen the show.) Parents remembered *Friends* as charming and funny with appealing characters. They just didn't remember that it was packed with sexual innuendo. (Common Sense Media recommends *Friends* for youth age 13+).[4] Parents in my workshops have also been stunned by doing the hatch mark exercise while watching the commercials during any major league sports event.

Guidelines for Facilitating a Porn-Free Childhood

Here are three steps you can take to help prevent your child from being exposed to sexual material that they're not ready for.

1) **Blinders off!** Be more aware of sexualized content in programs, movies, and advertisements (print and electronic)

that your child age two years and up may see. Get into the habit of skipping commercials or blocking online ads, and make sure that your toddler isn't watching the same programs that your tween and her homies are seeing. YouTube Kids, sadly, is still a minefield. Although it recently terminated thousands of videos and fifty channels that targeted children with violent/sexual/disturbing content, that content had already received billions of views. Stick to channels you know well until YouTube can do better in policing its videos for kids. Co-viewing, screen talk, and P&Q are some of your best allies in strengthening the bonds with your children so that they ask you about sexualized screen content instead of sneaking off to watch it. On the TV side, a huge number of shows each season, from *Black-ish* to *Scandal*, contain amazingly raunchy and explicit jokes and scenes—not to mention the Kardashians, Maury Povich, and scores of dodgy so-called "reality" shows. None of these are appropriate for very young children unless you want them to see "show and tell" about how to use a condom.

2) **Online resources!** There are a number of good websites that provide recommendations to help parents pick shows, movies, apps, and games. Use the resource provider that feels like the best fit for you, your values, and your children. I've provided a resource list in the Appendix. But for those who are deeply concerned about pornography's impact on children, I want to add one here: enough.org. The nonprofit organization behind the website Enough Is Enough provides resources for helping families understand how to make smart decisions online and keep kids safe from inappropriate or harmful material.

3) **Just talk about it.** Be available and willing to talk when your child starts asking questions, remind her of your family values, and ask some questions of your own. Here, I'm going to spare you the many parent-child dialogues I've heard and guided around sexual content or even nightly news. You do this your way—your family and your values are what count. Christine Koh, PhD, a scientist and founder and editor of the Boston Mamas parenting website (BostonMamas.com), is a big fan of not getting rattled if parents do find their children have seen something inappropriate. She believes, as I do, that kids shut down when parents overreact. If children are exposed to upsetting news, whether it's Pee-wee Herman or PewDiePie, your approach is the same. First, open up and generalize in gentle terms. In a case involving bias, you can use words like equality and accepting each other. In a case of sexual wrongdoing, talk about how we want to treat each other with respect and we don't touch other people in "private places." Then talk about the consequences of those actions. When someone does something he (or she) isn't supposed to do, there are consequences. Just remember to use your active listening skills. Or consult some good books.[5]

You may already be aware that boys as young as eight can successfully gain unlimited access to Internet porn. (Girls have access, too, but they use it less.) Again, this is something that needs our attention and compassion, not panic.

I'm not making the argument that kids should *never* see sexual content. I'm saying that there's a disconnection when tiny children constantly see highly sexual content without dialogue or discussion, followed by the abstinence lecture at age ten or eleven.

The Eye-Opening Research
of Dr. Gail Dines

Gail Dines, PhD, is a professor of sociology and women's studies at Wheelock College in Boston and is a pioneer in the study of pornography. A recipient of the Myers Center Award for the Study of Human Rights, Dr. Dines has written and spoken fervently about the hypersexualization of culture and how pornographic iconography has seeped into the media we all consume. Check out her TEDx talk, "Growing Up in a Pornified Culture," about what happens to young men when they grow up acclimated to porn. Here are four of the most damaging results she cites from ongoing porn use:

1) The appearance of a real girl is shocking to boys and men who've spent a lot of time with pornography. They're shocked by pubic hair, they're shocked by breasts that are less than perfect, or less than large. They have expectations and physical standards for women that are almost impossible and, many would say, undesirable to attain.

2) There is often violence of some kind associated with the way women are used in pornographic videos. The expectation that sexual interactions between men and women often incorporate violence toward women is destructive to male-female relationships.

3) There is zero emotional content in pornography and no assertion or implication that there may or should be feelings between the people having sex. If you strip emotion, tenderness, and commitment from the act of sex, how do you choose your partners? When and why would you marry or have children? Accepting pornography as the baseline for building relationships is like accepting child abuse as the basis for parenting skills. Given the porn epidemic, perhaps

it's not surprising that millennials are increasingly abstaining from sex, and fewer and fewer women view marriage as desirable, even in countries with strong marriage-focused traditions like Japan.[6]

4) Porn "stories" are largely transactional and they perpetuate a vicious fiction that women enjoy the kinds of things that are happening to them in these videos. For the record, a "transactional relationship" is one where all parties are out for themselves, and where the partners do things for each other expecting reciprocation. Sexual gifts or services are exchanged without emotional ties. (Writing this book, I was saddened to learn from Google that "almost all relationships start" from the transactional perspective. *Ouch.* Left undiscussed, that's a rather toxic starting point for your sexually curious tween.) Although her statistics and candor may set your teeth on edge, Dr. Dines does a particularly good job of challenging the myth that women enjoy the kind of sex you see in porn.

Since this book focuses on screen use in early childhood, it's best to stop here. I'm not an expert in childhood exposure to pornography and judging adults' private screen choices is well outside the scope of this book. But it's wise to notice that the fallout from children's exposure to "pornified" content is affecting our schools and our society because those effects are spreading. It's even better to remember that this is *our* world, people, and if we want to, we can change it. The surge of sexual harassment cases in 2017 signals that women and men everywhere are willing to take risks, come forward, and advocate for that change.

Chapter 8

Connecting Books and Movies

It's 7 PM, pajamas are on, teeth have been hurriedly brushed, and your child asks for *Goodnight Moon* as she heads for bed. Do you power-read straight through while your child lies there silently? Of course not! You use your best "story voice" and invite questions. You point to a character and ask who it is. Perhaps your child points to "the old lady" picture and tells you a story about a rabbit she saw in the yard. Perhaps she asks why a cow would jump over the moon. You laugh and talk together about the story and the pictures and you learn about how your child's mind works. Every time you read to your children, you're using the skills you're going to apply to screen time, starting with critical thinking skills. Let's look a little more closely at why reading stories to children is so effective in building parent-child relationships and neural networks.

George Gerbner was the first dean of the Annenberg Foundation, a family foundation that supports nonprofit organizations around the world. Almost twenty years ago Gerbner said, "There is

"There is no more serious business for a culture or a society than the stories we choose to tell our children."

no more serious business for a culture or a society than the stories we choose to tell our children."[1] As any early childhood teacher or parent of a young child will tell you, he was right. In addition to being intellectual catnip for our children, stories comprise our cultural connectivity, convey values, and provide individual and cultural role models. They are the mortar that holds our culture and civilization together. In his groundbreaking book, *Sapiens*, historian Yuval Noah Harari, PhD, states, "The real difference between us and chimpanzees is the mysterious glue that enables millions of humans to cooperate effectively. This mysterious glue is made of stories, not genes. We cooperate effectively with strangers because we believe in things like gods, nations, money, and human rights. Yet none of these things exists outside the stories that people invent and tell one another."[2]

Storytelling and narrative research have undergone a massive renaissance in recent years. Social scientists are studying the stories told by groups and communities, and psychologists study the connection between "stories of self" and the way individuals form their identities. Plus, the field of "organizational" storytelling is daily gaining traction in the business world.

Looking at the stories that people tell is an illuminating and powerful tool for coordinating and generating understanding. Sharing stories connects us and shapes us into communities. Stories are cultural engines whose motors drive the development of individual consciousness. Stories provide frameworks for interpretation, understanding, and meaning. Most important for children, stories are aspirational and motivational. But stories, especially those intended for very young children, don't and shouldn't operate in a vacuum or do all the developmental heavy lifting by themselves. Your interactions with children "around" (before, during, and after reading) story time add powerful new dimensions to the story and its effect on them. There is extraordinary potential to be realized from interacting with children while reading, telling, or watching stories.

As I've said before, reading a book to a child takes you both on an interactive odyssey and helps build your relationship. Questions are asked, opinions are shared, and both parties draw enjoyment from commenting on different parts of the story. Watching screen-based stories with children holds the same potential, provided we omit instructions to watch passively and quietly. And the sooner the better!

What I call *Mindful Viewing* is designed to capitalize on children's love of stories, screens, and sharing. In the next chapter I'll explore that further, but Mindful Viewing starts by elevating children's awareness of the story within the movie and their own responses to that story. As children continue to practice Mindful Viewing, they begin to notice, explore, and comment on the values and messaging reflected by the stories. Then they can start to make new meaning by offering new and different interpretations of the same story.

The earlier you introduce your children to critical thinking skills and Mindful Viewing, the better prepared they will be for the mesmerizing onslaught of news, games, stories, and social media. We live in a digital society and today's little ones are the second generation of digital natives. I've seen two-year-olds handle a smart phone as if they were born with one in their tiny hands. At first I thought I was seeing things when I noticed how adroit these tots are at manipulating the screen, selecting what they want to watch, and understanding how the device works. But here's the critical question: if they're smart and intuitive enough to understand at one- or two-years-old how that iPhone works, then why can't we assume they're also smart enough to *process what they're experiencing* on that iPhone, computer, tablet, or television screen? Because manipulating technology successfully has nothing to do with understanding its content. Not to worry, helping children understand content is where you, the parent, excel because you do it every night at story time.

Sharing the Reading Experience

Picture what happens at story time when a parent or teacher reads a book aloud to a child. Remember what we said earlier: the adult doesn't just plow through the story. When I'm reading a bedtime story, I sit on the bed and let the child snuggle. When I'm reading in a chair, I'll often have the child in my lap. So there's a tactile component, a physical closeness that elevates the feeling of intimacy, of being loved. In addition, children will often touch the book's pages or point to images, and show me a part of the story that they love, or ask a question about something that puzzles them. Children often ask me to go back and reread a favorite part of the book (especially if silly voices are involved), or they'll talk about a part of the book in relation to something that's happened in their own lives.

Every page of the story gives me the chance to ask questions. Sometimes, I'll point to an image and ask, "What color is that flower?" or "Why do you think the caterpillar was so hungry?" At the end of *Goodnight Moon*, my niece and I sometimes said good night to everything we could see in her room. Reading to a child is a highly interactive process that is often playful. Losing time for verbal interaction, shortchanging our kids on PAT, is part of the reason for the oft-quoted 30-million-word gap, which refers to a research study conducted by psychologists Betty Hart and Todd Risley.[3] Their study showed that children from lower-income families hear a staggering 30 million fewer words than children from higher-income families by the time they are four years old. Reading books aloud and practicing screen talk are two super-charged ways to close that 30-million-word gap.

Books Are Like Movies (or Apps or Games)

Think about what you're already doing with your child to prompt responses and insights when you're reading them a book. Then you do the exact same thing with a movie or an electronic game. The structure of the interaction is dictated by what you and the child notice together, by your and the child's imaginative responses to the story or the images on the screen. While the story may be linear and logical, good story *time* is not. It's full of fun and tangents, like collapsing in a fit of giggles. The child is learning vocabulary, gaining exposure to new ideas, and sharing delight and whimsy. Reading to a child is a multisensory experience that anchors story time to love and learning. The same thing can be said of screen time when you engage in screen talk.

Opening the Door to Dialogue

Because children will start noticing screens as soon as they see you using them, it's best to begin early to lay the foundation for an ongoing family dialogue around screen time. I recommend starting when your child is between two and three years old. We'll delve into this more deeply in later chapters and look at why from a neurological perspective this approach makes so much sense. For now, I want to walk you through how a book-based orientation to screen time might work. This is part of preparing your child to share his or her feelings about what they've seen.

Make sure that all visible screens have been turned off, including the television, computer, or tablet in the room. You don't want any distractions! Take your child on your lap with an open picture book. Point to several pictures in the book and say, "Sweetheart, what are these?"

First, she'll usually tell you what she physically sees in the pictures—a horse or a bird.

You say, "Yes, but there's one on each page. What do we *call* these?" Give her a clue if she needs help.

"Pictures," she says.

"All right," you say, "so these are pictures."

Then point to the words and ask, "What do we call these things?"

The whole process is interactive. Allow your child to figure it out herself, and provide *subtle* guidance if necessary, *without* making her feel as if you gave her the answer.

> The whole process is interactive. Allow your child to figure it out herself, and provide *subtle* guidance if necessary, *without* making her feel as if you gave her the answer.

"Those are words," she'll eventually say.

Next, point to the individual letters and ask, "What are these?"

Your child will probably say, "Those are letters."

Then ask her, "And what do the letters make?" Let her take ownership of the knowledge and allow her enough time to process.

"The letters make words," she'll say. Resist the urge to interrupt her or to jump in and help her mid-sentence. Staying the course here requires patience and confidence in your child.

Let's pause for a moment and examine what you've accomplished so far. Your child is on your lap and has separately identified pictures and words, successfully differentiating between both mediums. Continue on this same track with her. "Okay, there are pictures in a book." Then, point to the screen. "If we turn on a screen, will there be pictures?"

Let your child answer, "Yes."

Then ask, "Do you *like* watching those pictures?"

Usually a child will nod excitedly and sometimes want to talk about something she just saw. If the child wants to tell you something, take a moment to listen to what she says. At that point she may then say she wants to watch something or play a game. Tell her sweetly but firmly, "No, we're not going to turn on the screen now." Then, gesturing to the book and the screen say, "What's the difference between the pictures we see in the book and the pictures we see on the screen?" (Hint: If you point to the book when talking about the book and point to the screen when talking about the screen, these key ideas will be strongly retained by your child because you are providing aural, visual, and kinesthetic stimulation.)

Your little one is going to think about it for a minute and then pop out the answer that adults sometimes ponder and miss, "The pictures on the screen move."

If there is some hesitation and your child appears not to know, you can prompt with gentle hints by pointing to the screen and asking, "The pictures here do something special. What do they do? Are they just like the pictures in a book or are they different?" You can walk your index fingers across the screen as a hint, showing movement. You can whisper and act as if it's a secret, saying "The pictures . . ." The goal here is not to tell the answer but to let the child find the answer using the questions and cues you provide.

Compliment your child: "Yes, you're right, the pictures on the screen move, the pictures in the book don't! You're so smart!" Let them feel how proud you are. Your child has correctly distinguished between the pictures on a screen that move, and those in a book that do not. By identifying the fact that both books and screens show pictures, you've just helped your child make a connection between print media and screen text. That's a huge step, but it's also subtle, and it's really important.

Then smile and say, "I can tell you're getting excited because you said you wanted me to turn on the screen. Do you think that what you see on the screen is fun?"

At that point, take a moment to reinforce the child's articulation skills and the parent-child connection by saying, "Let's say that word together. Ready? '*Fun!*'"

Once the child has enjoyed saying the word with you, ask again, "Do you think that what you see on the screen is fun?"

If she nods, indicating "yes," ask her what's fun about watching the screen.

If she shakes her head "no," ask her what's *not* fun about it.

Follow your child's cues. She may tell you different things. Sometimes a child will say "It makes me laugh," or "I see colors," or she'll tell you about a show she likes, or something she saw that frightened her.

You may also have to prompt her: "Do you like the colors?" or "Is there somebody, a character, that you really like?" I'll start introducing that language as early as I can, even with a two-year-old. You can ask, "Who do you like best on *Sesame Street*?"

"I like Cookie Monster . . . "

Consider this. After only a couple of questions, your child has internalized that there are words and pictures in books, pictures on screens, and that those pictures move. While we adults may take this type of knowledge for granted, these are core constructs that, unless taught, children don't automatically understand. I encourage you to ask other questions, too, during these sessions. For example, "Are there words on screens, too? Do we see words or do we hear words?" Posing simple questions and then actively listening makes you a caring and trusted mentor in your child's eyes instead of a grouchy old media warden who "won't let me watch what I want." That's a significant shift in the family dynamic around screen time right there.

By the next session, your child will know what to expect. Choose a different book this time, point to a picture, and ask, "What are these again?" Sometimes the child will say, "Mommy, read me the story." Go ahead and read a little bit or all of it, that's fine, too.

"What did we say yesterday that these are called?" you ask.

"That's a giraffe."

"Yes, that's a giraffe, but these are on every page, what are they?"

"Oh, those are pictures!"

"And what are these?"

"Mommy, those are words!"

"Good, are we going to see pictures if we turn that screen on?"

"Yes, and they move."

"And yesterday you said it was . . . " (cue her with an *F* sound).

"Fun!"

At that point, your child may tell you something she wants to watch on the screen. You can nod to acknowledge her request without saying she can watch, and then go right back to asking her simple questions, remembering what we've said about approach, tone, and tempo. Often, at that point, I'll ask, "So what have you seen on a screen that you thought was fun?" I'll do the arm movement and then let the child tell me about a show or a video that she thought was fun.

As soon as she's finished, I continue, "But have you ever seen anything that was totally different from what Mommy or Grandma said was good? If it's not good, what is it? It could be . . . ?"

Let your child find the word. Some children come out with "naughty" or "mean." Great! Just lead them to "bad."

"What's a short word for naughty or mean . . . a word that begins with the letter B?"

If he can't get the word out, then say, "It could be bad. Have you seen things that were bad?" If you ask this in an accusing or judgmental tone, right away he'll clam up. Your body language and the sound of your voice must be encouraging and kind. Remember, children

Remember, children like to talk about what they've seen and often they're amazed that Mom or Dad is interested in their screen experiences.

like to talk about what they've seen and often they're amazed that Mom or Dad is interested in their screen experiences.

Keep going. Maintain the dialogue. "Honey, what have you seen on a screen that was bad?" You may hear from your little one that he saw pushing, kicking, hitting, or killing, or that he heard yelling and screaming, or a naughty word. Let him tell you everything he can remember, nodding lovingly and not judging, just listening supportively. Continuing, you say, "Okay, wait a minute, you said it was fun *(gesture)* to watch the screen, but you just told me we can also see things on screens that are bad. So . . . what about things that are sad?" Sometimes your child will go right into a story about sad things he saw a screen. If he does, just listen compassionately. If you sense that your child is ready to stop, table the lesson until later.

"So, my goodness, it can be fun to watch screens, but we can also see things that are bad or sad. Wow, I think we should talk about it some more; maybe we'll talk about it again tomorrow."

It's fine if a day or two passes before the next session. You should be as consistent as possible, but it should also be natural and organic, never forced. You'll know when the window is right. Each time, go through the whole process again, perhaps varying it by letting the child fill in the answer when you pause: "These are *(pictures)*; these are *(words)*; on a screen what do pictures do?" Always use the same question-and-answer format and you can branch out to other questions. "So what did you see on a screen that was fun yesterday?" Let your child answer each time. "What about bad . . . did you see anything that was bad on a screen?" If there's a slight hesitation, be patient and encouraging, and keep maintaining eye contact. "What about sad?"

Then you move on to the last question, "Have you seen anything on a screen that was scary?" Here, you'll almost always find some surprises. You may discover that your child was frightened by something you had no idea was scary to her, or that she saw something awful you didn't know she'd seen. I'll include more tips on this below. At the close of the talk, remember to keep your tone soft and use an endearment because you're about to open a new door and you want it to be inviting. You're going to tie everything together and communicate unequivocally your willingness to talk with your child about what she's seen.

"So we know that what we see on screens can be fun," you say. "But you also told me that you saw things that were bad or sad or scary. Sweetie, when you see something that's bad or sad or scary, I want you to come and talk to me. Anytime you see something that makes you feel scared or sad or upset, we can talk about it."

Beyond Scary

This whole interaction, laying the foundation for dialogue, takes five minutes a day or less. A suggestion—if there's been a gap between sessions of more than a few days, it's better not to lead with bad, sad, or scary. Instead, recommence on a positive note with fun. With very young children, it's always good to use gestures, too. You can put your arms way up in the air with the hands straight to say things can be fun, and then make two fists and put them on your lap to indicate bad, and then let the child say it with you. Then put two index fingers under your eyes to indicate tears and say "sad," and then raise your shoulders and move your hands to visually express scary.

A friend of my mother's told me that, when she was a little girl, she was frightened by the wicked queen in the movie *Snow White*. She said that she never told anyone about her experience because

her babysitter told her she wasn't "supposed to be scared by movies."
When you ask your child what they've seen on a screen that was scary,
this can be a big test for you as a parent. If you want to encourage
dialogue and honest disclosure from your child, you can't freak out
with questions like, "Where on earth did you see *Scream?*" If your
child tells you he saw *Chucky* or *Halloween* with his older cousins, you
need to avoid getting upset and yelling, "Who let you watch that?"
Just keep that smile on your face without a flicker of discomfort and
focus on how your child *felt*: "Wow, I would have been scared, honey,
were you? What did you see that was scary?"

By all means make a mental note to talk to the adult who allowed
the viewing, but do not say anything to your child that evinces your
distress. Simply ask open-ended questions that allow him to tell you
what he saw and how he felt about it.

"Wow, you saw someone with a white mask like when people play
hockey? What was scary about it?"

"Well," replies your child, "there was screaming and blood and . . ."

Let him tell you. *Breathe.*

Often when a child talks about being scared by what they've seen,
I'll ask, "Did it give you nightmares?" Sometimes your child will say
he had nightmares, sometimes he won't. And sometimes he may
be too paralyzed by the memory to say anything. That's the perfect
opportunity to gently hug him or take him on your lap, grab hold
of both his hands, and quietly repeat, "You know what, when you
see anything that's scary, you can always come talk to me." At other
times, it may take action to break through the barrier of nightmares.
I'll suggest a remedy that works well with children in art therapy.
At a Catholic school in California, during the initial dialogue I've
just outlined, a little boy named Nathan quietly confided to me that
he had a nightmare that "wouldn't go away," and "put pictures" in
his mind.

I told him, "It might help if you drew a picture of the part of the movie that scares you the most. Then we can rip it up and it will be gone."

The next day, he came in proudly, bringing a picture of a monster that he wanted to show me and his whole kindergarten class. He said, "Miss Nicole, it worked! I drew this with my daddy and I'm not scared anymore."

One year later, I shared this same approach with a group of kindergarten students who had seen zombies, vampires, monsters, and, of course, *Chucky*. The next day, when I asked if anyone had drawn a picture of what scared them, a shy little boy raised his hand. He said, "I drew a picture but I didn't rip it up. I put my picture on a pillow and I punched the pillow." Everyone laughed and clapped, and his idea became a core part of our approach.

The goal is to break the old mold of "media policing" and create a new way of interacting with our children around screen time, one that will support rather than erode family dynamics. Instead of catalyzing conflict, parents' new role during screen time will be rooted in becoming caring mentors who can mediate their children's experiences with screens. The priming exercise opens the door to that new role because it culminates in an invitation: "If you see something that is fun or bad or sad or scary, I want you to know that you can come talk to me." This is a powerful invitation that will allow you to build a completely new relationship with your children around screen time.

> The goal is to break the old mold of "media policing" and create a new way of interacting with our children around screen time, one that will support rather than erode family dynamics.

Of course, if you instruct your children to *report* their responses to screen time, they won't enjoy the process or look forward to it. If you give them the opportunity to share their responses in a caring, supportive environment where their answers drive the discussion, the dialogues and disclosures can be magical.

Going Deeper—
Purpose and Messaging

The purpose of story-based or narrative media is primarily entertainment. But from gender roles to life values, narrative content is imbued with cultural messaging. In early childhood, stories carry a powerful potential to engender behavioral programming. We can free children from the dangers of unconscious absorption of undesirable values (and erroneous conclusions) just by getting into the habit of talking about our responses to what we're watching once or twice a week. Again, you don't need to do this every time you turn on a screen. But a family culture that invites children to respond and give their opinions, a family culture that

> We can free children from the dangers of unconscious absorption of undesirable values (and erroneous conclusions) just by getting into the habit of talking about our responses to what we're watching once or twice a week.

values children's responses and that uses language to strengthen their intellectual abilities, is a life-changing asset.

I'm not suggesting that parents need to take over for schools and fill gaps that teachers are missing. To thrive in today's demanding pre-K and kindergarten classrooms, our children need all the help they can get! We can naturally fill in some of those gaps just by engaging children in talking about their experiences with screen content. What better use for the hours we all spend with screens?

Story-based screen content is especially rich and productive for strengthening literacy skills, higher-order thinking, social-emotional learning, and giving us, as parents, a real finger on the pulse of how our children are developing. You can learn more in one twenty-minute co-viewing session than you can in six months of taking your kids to the movies, sitting there, and walking out asking, "Did you like it?" You're already putting in the time. You're just not leveraging the time investment that you've already made. Making small, strategic changes in the ways you're talking to your children and including screen time in your discussion can yield extraordinary outcomes.

In schools, I promise very young children that if they use their energy and concentration when watching screens, if they pay attention to character, plot, and setting, if they notice what they're feeling and thinking, and if they talk about the details of what they're viewing, *they will get smarter.* Think about it. If all the cognitive constructs I've listed are activated during viewing, then getting smarter is almost inevitable, simply because they're watching so much. If you start using the cerebral cortex instead of the limbic system for even 20 percent of the time that you're viewing screens, your neural networks will grow, your perceptivity will grow, your ability to express yourself will grow, your ability to notice things in a text will grow, and your ability to notice your own responses (metacognition) will grow. It would be impossible for all those things to grow without getting smarter.

After children are comfortable with character, plot, and setting, and you can easily introduce those words into the dialogue, you can start using words that refer to the structure and sequence of the plot: beginning, middle, and end, and problem and solution. Even talking after the child watches something alone gives you hundreds of opportunities. At the end of a video, a child may say, "I really liked it." That's your cue to ask: "What did you like about the story? Did you like the beginning, the first part? Or the middle? Or the last part, the ending?" Then: "Why did you like that part?" Just do that a few times when talking about what you've seen together.

If your child is in kindergarten and headed toward first grade, you can introduce problem and solution into the dialogue the same way. During co-viewing, just pause for a moment and say, "Uh oh. I think that character has a problem. What's the problem?" Whether the problem is a locked door, a lost lunch, or a crabby crossing guard, your brilliant child will know the answer.

Then ask, "So the character needs a solution. What could he do?" Pause for a response. Occasionally including the words *problem* and *solution* in your dialogue about books or screen stories gives another boost to higher-order thinking skills.

Continuing with literacy constructs, it's easy to move on to talk about the main idea of a movie. I often ask, "What was the *main* idea of the movie? What was it about?" Pause for a second to let that sink in, then ask, "Can you tell me in one sentence?"

The first few times, you'll almost certainly have to guide your child gently away from telling you the entire plot in the popular "and then" form. But the main idea can and should be subjective for little ones and there are no wrong answers. When you're opening the door to the main idea, and asking children to tell you the main idea of the movie in one sentence, it's a challenge for their brains! So enjoy what they come up with.

For example, after seeing Michael Sporn's *Goodnight Moon*, a class of three- and four-year-olds told me:

"We can be quiet to sleep."
"If I look at stuff in my room, it can put me to sleep."
"A bunny is quiet."
"Grandmas look like bunnies."

After seeing *Frozen* (for the tenth time) in a school where recess had been canceled, a group of third-graders shared their thoughts on the main idea of the film:

"You should love your sister."

"Snowmen can be big or little."

"Reindeers are funny."

"If you love someone enough, you will do anything to help them."

Whether you're talking about books or movies or TV shows, keep the main idea simple and accessible and personal.

Now that you're expertly insinuating complex literacy concepts into fun dialogues with your children, you can start asking questions that allow them to infer how the story, character, or setting changes over time. Here's an example.

"When the movie started, what season (or part of the year) was it?"

"What's a season?" Here you have a choice. You can tell the child, "Seasons are winter, spring, summer, fall." Or you can practice your Socratic questioning skills, and prompt inferential reasoning.

"Okay, where we live, if everything is green and it's hot and we have our bathing suits on, what time of year is that?"

You or the child: "Summer!"

Instead of just telling them what *season* is, ask a "self-to-world" question that connects their real-life experience to the answer. You don't have to go through all four seasons. After one or two questions, you can say, "The seasons are the time of year."

Asking a question that includes clues will allow children the fun of searching for the answer themselves. If a child discovers the answer herself, like any successful explorer, she gains a tremendous

> If a child discovers the answer herself, like any successful explorer, she gains a tremendous sense of accomplishment along with better retention of the answer.

sense of accomplishment along with better retention of the answer. Authentic ownership of one's core learning experiences is incredibly empowering and is an essential ingredient in cultivating independent thinkers. But of course, picking the times to ask those questions instead of giving a direct answer is up to the parent. Timing is everything and if your child is on his last nerve, don't make him answer yet another question. If the child genuinely doesn't know, then, of course, you can tell him the answer!

Long story short, character, plot, and setting are all part of helping children build a healthier relationship with media and screens.

First, they build neural networks.

Second, they are tools to propagate habits of questioning.

Third, they allow the child to build a more refined vocabulary of words and experiences with respect to the actions and qualities of characters, the events that happen in a plot, the ending of a story, and the main idea. To borrow from feng shui, those three words become the earthly branches from which myriad heavenly stems can emerge.

Chapter 9

Psychological Priming

When Malcolm Gladwell wrote about psychological priming in *Blink*, it confirmed my belief that priming could be an incredibly useful tool to prepare very young children for screen time. In psychological priming, what you think or talk about before you take action can influence your experience and the outcome of that action. Offering an elegant description of priming in *The Social Animal*, David Brooks states, "A perception cues a string of thoughts that alter subsequent behavior." For example, test subjects who are asked to read a series of words like "assisted living," "retirement," or "ancient" will walk more slowly exiting the room than entering it. Before I read *Blink* I had already been using a form of priming with elementary and high-school age audiences at the Chicago International Children's Film Festival.

Many festivals have preprogram announcements, usually a form of oral "housekeeping" where you thank your sponsors or tell the audience that there's going to be a director present after the screening.

What I did was completely different. Each year, I wrote scripts to prime the mental pump of each child in the audience before the screening started. But rather than priming with single words, preshow scripts were structured to prime by surprising children, re-directing their attention, and inviting them to think and feel in new ways.

Here's a playful distillation of that message for younger children, minus all the pauses, energy, and encouraging inflections:

"You can't just come to a festival to watch a movie; you need to learn how to watch a movie. Were you born knowing how to read a book? Someone had to teach you, right? Well, just like books, movies are made up of many parts. There's so much going on in every moment: the music, the pictures, the story, the special effects. So let's learn how to watch a movie."

> "The most important part of a movie is what's happening in your own mind."

The script was interactive and it moved quickly toward, "When we're watching a movies, there are two places where there is a lot going on. One is here *(pointing to the screen)*. Where else is there a lot going on *(pointing to the head)*? The most important part of a movie is what's happening in your own mind."

In writing these scripts, I didn't view myself as an adult expert. Instead I focused on children as experienced viewers who had seen thousands and thousands of hours of screen content. My goal was to make the screening a vehicle for them to actualize that huge body of information and expertise so they could gain greater enjoyment, understanding, and self-awareness as twenty-first century learners.

Those scripts were used with thousands and thousands of children by hundreds of facilitators whom I trained. The words were only effective in concert with the right tone, attitude, and energy while making consistent eye contact in reaching out to that audience. Over time, I learned that there were hundreds of ways to prime effectively and there is no one ideal priming script. But the basic ingredients include affirming the child as an expert, framing a challenge in a new and fun way, and directing focus inwardly, as well as outwardly toward the film.

Festival screenings and post-screening discussions became staggeringly successful in prompting critical thinking and profound insights, as well as thousands of written comments from teachers, parents, and children. Film directors who were present for the pre-show priming often asked, "Why doesn't everyone do this at festivals?"

Reading about psychological priming inspired me to take that idea even further. What if we could prime very young children for a full complement of developmental responses and interactions before they started viewing? Because my goal was to develop a priming process for early childhood, I wanted to integrate visual, kinesthetic, and auditory prompts that would best facilitate children's fullest engagement. One of the operative questions was: "Can we make viewing a single short video or app into an accelerative learning experience?" Based on feedback and responses from teachers, we were able to accomplish just that.

Here's a script that walks you through the usual opening for a festival. Although the approach with very young children is slightly different, this one gives parents and teachers of elementary schoolchildren a few useful nuggets.

"Welcome to the festival! You are here to do something really exciting and important. Today we're going to see ten films from nine different countries, and we're going to award a prize to the film that gets the most votes . . . from you! So while you're watching, you need to be thinking about all the different films and comparing them against each other in your minds. That's a challenge! But I know you can do it. So while we're watching, we're going to think about what we like *(pause)*, what we don't like *(pause)*, and why. Let's say it together!

What we like *(pause)*, what we don't like *(pause)*, and why. Do we think we can do that?

"But if we're going to remember all the movies, characters, and all the things that happen in all those movies, we've got to wake up our minds! Do you know the best way to wake up our minds quickly? *Energy.* That's what we're going to use. But we're not going to get up and run around the block, we're going to just use the energy in our hands. Let's put our hands up! We're going to do something called the 'shake-stop.' When I shake my hands, you're going to shake yours, and when I stop, you'll stop with me."

Immediately you'll notice the energy level, the excitement, and the focus increasing in the room. We'll do the shake-stop five or six times, and then sometimes ask a child who is very energized and focused to come forward to lead a couple of shake-stops. At the end, I'll ask the students, "Can you feel your energy?" Since they've just been moving their hands with a lot of energy, their pulses will have accelerated, they can feel the blood moving through their bodies, and they can feel it in their hands. So they're going to feel an elevation of energy. And once they feel that energy, I'll say, "We use our energy and concentration to keep our minds awake."

When I say the word *energy* I do a mini-movement with my hands. When I say *concentration*, I'll put my index and middle fingers on my temples. Then when I say, "to keep our minds awake," I make two loose fists, put them on either side of my head, and open my hands when I say the word *awake*. I do that very quickly and it becomes a game. "We use our energy and concentration to keep our minds awake." That's a powerful but very simple cue that tells children that they are going to need to watch in a special way. The process is very simply concluded by saying, "Are we ready? Are we ready to watch the movie?"

The result is that children move into viewing with an empowered understanding of what it means to watch movies, supported by a boost of physical energy that is going to keep their minds active, and with the engaging challenge to notice qualities and characteristics about each film that will allow them to pick a favorite. So they are not watching as consumers, they're watching as critics.

The evidence of such a festival screening speaks for itself. You see children who have never watched a foreign or subtitled film before enjoying the content, reading the text, and making text-to-self connections that compare their lives with the lives of the children they are seeing in the films. Intellectually, this is a very high-level set of interactions with an audiovisual text. And the children are enjoying themselves! While the benefits of introducing children to global culture and concepts outside of their experience are clear, you've also hit a dynamic reset button. By priming their screen experience before it happens, you can fundamentally transform the way children interact with one of the most powerful influences in their lives: digital devices.

The Four Steps to Priming for Young Children

For a two-year-old or a three-year-old, the priming process should be a bit more detailed. The priming still moves quickly, but you take more time with the enquiry-based approach I'll outline next. As suggested before, you'll want to pick a supportive setting for your first "screen priming" experience and be aware of your tone of voice and demeanor. You'll also incorporate movements and gestures and use questions to make the learning process lively and interactive.

Checklist for Priming
✓ Positive setting
✓ Upbeat or playful tone of voice and demeanor
✓ Simple movements or gestures to accompany words

✓ Ask questions rather than telling children what to do or
providing answers

It's important not to make this overly serious, or a directive with
the child. Priming a child at age three to seven to make the most of
viewing screens should have the same overall feeling of happy anticipation that the child has just before you start reading him or her a
story. With a very young child, perhaps a two-year-old, you may want
to be slightly more instructional and have them follow you a little
more closely. At any age, keep a screen handy, whether it's a tablet, a
phone, or a big screen TV, but make sure that you're looking at the
child and she's focused on you before you start.

Step 1: Have Fun Identifying Screens

I often start by pointing or holding out a screen and asking, "What's
this called?" At first the child will tell me what kind of screen I'm holding. She may say, "It's a phone!" or "It's an iPad!" I'll point to the actual
screen and ask, "What's this part of the phone called?" If she doesn't
know, I'll say the word *screen* and then we'll repeat that word together.

Then I'll ask, "How many different kinds of screens do we have at
home?" After pausing for a moment, I'll suggest, "Let's find them and
count them!" Then we'll run through the house making a game nam-
ing all the different kinds of screens and counting them. At the end,
we'll sit together, and I say, "Wow, we counted a lot of screens and a lot
of different kinds of screens." Immediately I'll ask my next question.

Step 2: Separate Screen from Self,
Introduce Screen Smart

"So, where does everything we see on a screen go?"

An adult might read that question and think, "The question
doesn't make sense. If I'm watching a movie or playing a game, the

image disappears and is replaced by a new image. If I'm working on a computer, the answer depends on the software I'm using." But a young child will be intrigued by this question, especially when we ask with an air of positive anticipation. We're asking them to be aware that everything we watch on screens ends up in our minds. But we're not going to *tell them that* and preempt their discovery. It's important for children to grasp the priming progression for themselves, and notice that information appears on a screen and enters our minds.

Nicole: "We see lots of things on screens. Where do they go?" Even if I think children know the answer I'm seeking and they're starting to tell me, I keep asking questions to keep the interaction playful and creative.

Nicole: "Do they fall on the floor? Do they fly out the window? Where do they go?" I may start tapping my forehead or my temple to give a hint. Then a small avalanche of answers will pour out.

"They go in your brain." "Things go in your mind."

One five-year-old told me that "pictures and ideas go in your eyes and up to your brain."

Nicole: "Wow, so everything we see and hear on screens ends up in our minds?" *Nodding.* "That's a lot of stuff." More nodding.

Nicole: "I don't know about you, but I don't think I *want* things getting into my mind that I don't like or understand." At this point, my expression will look quizzical and a little troubled.

Nicole: "Do we really want to let *everything* from screens into our minds?" As soon as children decide that letting "everything" into their minds might be a bad idea, I introduce the final concept in this learning progression.

Nicole: "So if we don't want to let *every*thing into our minds, we need to notice what's getting in. We need to be Screen Smart! Let's say that: Screen Smart! To be Screen Smart I need to keep my *mind awake.* Let's learn how to keep our minds awake!"

There are much longer versions of this priming progression for first- and second-graders. I might ask them what happens when "too much" stuff gets into their minds, or ask if they think it's possible to watch screens too much. When they tell me that, yes, they think it's possible to watch too much, I ask how they feel when they watch too much. The kinds of answers that come pouring out can make you laugh and cry. I've been told:

> "Things get stuck in here *(pointing to his head)!*"
> "I think I was sleeping with my eyes open."
> "It's embarrassing because I drool."
> "I get more scared and can't turn off the screen in my head."

But, as a three-year-old told me, the key point is this: "Stuff gets into our minds and we need to know what it is."

Step 3: Connect Energy and Concentration to Screen Time

I've used energy and concentration priming in a hundred ways. Sometimes, I've just used the words and let children infer what energy and concentration are from the gestures I'm using. At other times, I've unfolded the terms in layers of communications that we call *scaffolding sets* because they scaffold—that is, build upon—very quickly between ideas, movements, concepts, and new vocabulary. Here's an example of a scaffolding set that's been used with thousands of children.

Parent: "We're going to use our energy! Do you know what energy is? What's energy?"

If your child hasn't heard the word before, you can use this as a vocabulary-building moment, and encourage her to say it with you. Then continue by offering a short definition or—my preference—by asking questions that allow the child to build an understanding of the word herself.

Parent: "What do we have to put into a car so it can move?"

Child: "Gas."

Parent: "Right! So gas is the energy a car needs to move." (If you own a Volt or a Tesla, you may have already taught your child the word *electricity*. Use the example that best serves what your child knows.)

Parent: "What do you need so you can move?" (Sometimes I mime eating here.)

Child: "Food!"

Parent: "Right, so food gives us energy. Energy helps us move. So let's move now. Show me your energy!"

Then hold your hands up with fingers straight, and your palms flat facing each other. Relaxing your wrists, shake your hands using a lot of energy. Shake them for two or three seconds, just shaking continuously not doing any specific rhythm. Then stop suddenly with the hands held straight up as they were when you started. The child will follow you, probably giggling.

Then continue "Shake . . . and stop! Can you stop with me, at the exact time I stop? Okay. Shake . . . and stop! We're using our energy! Shake! Stop!"

Then you point to your head: "And we're using our focus!" You can say "focus" if that word feels more accessible for your child developmentally, and if you think your child is ready to learn a new word with several syllables, you can say "concentration."

"And we're going to use concentration! Let's say that: *concentration!*"

And I almost always put my hands up, and use two fingers to tap my temples when I say the word *concentration,* tapping once for each syllable and widening my eyes a little. We practice the word a couple of times with energy. It's fun to say those words with Mommy and Daddy!

Then you'll want to make sure the child understands what *focus* or *concentration* is.

"Hey, do you know what focus is?" you ask in an encouraging tone. Make sure to pause and keep a smile on your face whether she knows the word or not. If the child doesn't know, you can say, "Focus is when we pay attention. When you use your *whole mind* to do something." Then you go back to the movements. "Okay, we're going to shake and stop! Shake. And stop! And that means we're using our energy *(circle the palms a little bit)* and our concentration."

Step 4: Keeping Our Minds Awake

At this point your child may be laughing. She may think you're doing the silliest thing ever! When that happens, I enjoy the laughter with a smile, then look at the child and say one more time, "We use our energy and our concentration *(pause for emphasis)* to keep our minds awake!"

When you say the words "to keep," make a loose fist with both hands and put those loose fists on both sides of your head close to your temples. When you say the word, "awake," just open your hand quickly. "Mind awake!" Then say, "Let's do that together" and repeat the movement and the words, "To keep our minds awake!" One more time, "To keep our minds awake!"

Sometimes I'll say, "Now let's put it all together," and do the entire sentence again with movements. "We're going to use our energy" (with palms held out straight, facing each other you make a choo choo train motion, like the wheels on a train making tiny circles), "and our concentration" (using the index finger and the middle finger of both hands), tap your temples on each syllable of the word "concentration" or "focus."

Finally, say, "To keep our minds awake." (Place loose fists on the temples, letting them spring open on the word "awake.")

If you think your child is losing focus, just go back to the shake-stop exercise because that's always fun. As you continue, if they really

love shake-stop and want to keep doing it, you can make it more challenging by saying "Shake," and then stopping (with a lot of energy)
without warning, like a game of statues. At that point, the child is
learning to respond first to an aural cue, then to a visual cue, so you're
stimulating different parts of the brain with a single fun exercise. At
the end of shake-stop, you'll want to add, "We're using our energy and
our concentration to keep our minds awake!"

After we've reviewed the exercise, I say, "When we watch (or when
we play the game), we're going to keep our minds awake. And after
we watch, we're going to talk about it!" When I say, "talk about it," I
hold up my hand and use the universal gesture for talking. My four
fingers are on top, my thumb is on the bottom, and I touch my thumb,
moving my fingers up and down.

At age one-and-a-half or two, you don't need to explain to a child
why you want them to "talk about it." They'll just be happy to talk
about it. You wouldn't need to explain to a child that you're going to
be reading them a story. They know you're going to be reading them
a story because they can't read. So when you say, "We're going to talk
about it," they'll want to talk about it! They want to talk with you.
You're offering extra time with Daddy, time during which the child
knows she'll have your full attention. Talking with you is a bonus,
another fun part of screen time. With this one sentence, you're setting
up an incredibly simple but powerful (and fun!) set of behavioral
expectations for your child:

> First, that viewing requires effort from me
> Second, that I get to talk to my Mommy, Daddy, or any adult with
>   whom I am watching
> Third, that there are expectations of me during screen time

After you've shared the energy and concentration exercise a couple
of times, you can start using pauses to cue the child. For example, I

might want to prime quickly by saying, "We're going to turn on the screen and when we do, we're going to see a lot of different things! I want you to be able to tell me about it, so what do we need to do? Keep our minds awake! And how are we going to do that? We'll use our . . ." And pause. *Let them say the word energy.* Your pause will give them the chance to verbally put that part of the puzzle in place. This makes it participatory and satisfying, like knowing the words to a song.

"Energy!"

"And our . . ." (pause, pointing to your head and let the child fill in concentration or focus). (Note: When you point to your head, the child may say "Your brain, your mind!" Redirect by saying, "Yes, we're going to use our brains to . . ." pause and if they don't come up with focus or concentrate, give them a hint by saying the first letter of the word.)

When they've said concentrate or focus, ask: "What are we going to use our energy and concentration for?"

Then cue them visually by putting the loose fists at your temples. If they don't respond, prompt them with "to keep . . . " When the child says "my mind awake," open your hands and encourage her to do the movement with you, by saying, "Let's do it together!" Early on, a very young child may start to wonder about what keeping their mind awake is about. They may just think it is about not falling asleep. And sometimes children will say, "Mommy, I'm going to stay awake!"

You can gently instruct with, "Oh, but we need to keep our *minds* awake! Your mind is so special. When your mind is awake, it helps you notice all the different parts of the movie/show/app."

As the child gets more comfortable and familiar with the expectation of staying alert and noticing details and being aware of her body while using a screen, it can be helpful to revisit "where everything on a screen goes" as a means of inspiring her to be consistently mindful. The beauty of this simple technique is that children themselves often come to their own conclusions and take action. Many parents have reported children saying, "If I'm watching a screen and my mind is asleep, I shouldn't be watching!" Or even better, "I'm not being Screen Smart, Mommy, let's turn it off."

Although it takes several pages to describe, the whole process takes no more than two to three minutes. It's based on a simple premise that using digital devices mindfully and with alertness is something children will choose to do themselves whether they're watching story-based content or playing with apps and video games. When they participate in the priming progression, children can feel their energy and they can feel the difference when they use screens with and without energy. They understand "sleep watching." They know how they feel after "letting everything get into their minds" and they're motivated to protect themselves. Seriously. No one wants to think that stuff gets into their minds that they don't know about.

Precious Moments:
Before the Screen Goes On

As a festival director, I had watched several hundred festival screenings before I realized that the most magical and productive time for brain development is the moment just *before* the movie (DVD, TV, game, virtual reality or VR, or YouTube program) starts. Just before they begin viewing, children feel high anticipation and positive excitement that holds great potential developmentally. But too often, those rarified moments are lost by simply pressing play, passing back a phone, or keeping our kids calm with popcorn, candy, and soda before the movie starts. We expect to sit and be quiet and watch for as long as we can, and then get up and leave. Sometimes we eat during screen time, perhaps laugh or cry, but the scope and even the possibility of human interaction is drastically curtailed when we sit in front of screens. And although gaming and even VR are more interactive, ignoring the moments before engaging the screen still carries the same burden of lost potential.

One of my favorite stories about a first-time moviegoer happened at a festival screening. After the lights went down, the two-year-old daughter of Jennifer Farrington, President of the Chicago Children's Museum whispered, "Mommy, when the lights go on will we be in California?" When Jennifer spoke with her daughter she discovered that the toddler thought they were on an airplane!

We adults haven't spent a lot of time thinking about what could happen in the moments before a child engages a screen. I can still hear parents asking, "Prescreen time? Is that even a thing?" Yep, it's a thing, and you're going to be so glad when you start using it differently. The fifteen to ninety seconds of prescreen time are your very own, magical "control button" allowing you to determine how you and your children will be affected by screens and technology. Activating the potential of prescreen time gives you access to new parts of your brain, new outcomes, new ways of relating to your children and one another. It's a gateway to the promised land of technology. Best of all, you're the gatekeeper. Mindfully crossing the threshold of engagement also helps end the entrenched, consumer passivity that we endure with respect to engaging screen content.

> The fifteen to ninety seconds of pre-screen time are your very own, magical "control button" allowing you to determine how you and your children will be affected by screens and technology.

Keeping Our Minds Awake

After your child has participated enthusiastically in the full priming progression at least ten times, it's possible to cue them with short statements.

"Okay, we're going to be Screen Smart!" Or, "We're going to start watching when we know we can be Screen Smart!" Or, "You told me you felt so much better when you keep your mind awake. So if we start sleep watching and our minds are asleep, what should we do?"

Or "When we watch, we need to keep *(pause to let them say 'our minds awake')*, and if we don't we're going to stop watching!" Smile! You're not making a threat. A child will understand that in the same way that a child begins to understand that, "Wow, if there's a lot of sun, it's bright, and it's summer, it can be hot outside. Well, if I'm watching a screen, without using energy or concentration, and my mind is asleep, I shouldn't be watching!"

It's important to know that there is no single correct order for doing the energy and concentration priming, and the shake-stop. You can use those exercises to re-prime as needed whenever you notice focus flagging in any activity, not just screen talk.

If your child has trouble with the shake-stop for some reason, you can also use quick, high-energy, rhythmic clapping patterns. The one that's easiest and most effective is "one, two, one-two-three." Parents, teachers, caregivers, and even pediatric nurses use this sound pattern to gain children's attention and involvement. It involves rhythmic clapping where the beats are slow, slow, quick, quick, quick. When using rhythmic clapping to boost energy, you'll do it for only ten or fifteen seconds—a very short time. You just need enough of the sound and movement pattern to lift the child's energy and focus. Once the child has that beat, you can vary and play with the rhythms for pure fun.

Just remember that after raising her energy level, it's important to get the child's focus and make eye contact in a supportive way prior to turning on the screen, or handing the child a screen to use independently. Also, whether you are co-viewing or simply priming the child for solo viewing, you'll want to add, "After we watch, we're going to talk about it."

Right away, you've infused viewing with a new level of accountability. Think about your own screen time. If you're watching mindlessly or playing with two screens at once, you won't remember anything and you'll just shrug if someone asks you about what you've seen. The point is that giving children actual "jobs" before they start watching supports cognitive function. Yet it's not difficult and it in no way impedes their enjoyment of viewing, provided you don't give them the same job repeatedly or with an overly serious tone of voice. Again, you're habituating them to expect to notice, think, and talk about details during their viewing. This promotes neural networks, builds their vocabulary, and improves their communication skills as you engage them in conversation around their digital devices.

Energetic Movement Supports Brain Function

In case you're curious about my inclusion of physical exercises, plosives, and hand movements among Screen Smart skills, there is some fascinating research that demonstrates higher levels of learning and achievement are tied to physical exercise and movement.[1] I developed these energy and concentration boosters long before recent research was available, and had used them in hundreds of schools before including them in the Screen Smart approach. But there were other reasons for wanting to "physicalize" children's interactions with technology. Like millions of others, I was appalled to read about young people who had died after gaming for twenty-six to thirty-six hours straight. The young men were so apparently focused on their games that they forgot about their bodies.[2] These are extreme examples, but they highlighted a real need for physical awareness during interactions with technology. So in developing the Screen Smart program, I also wanted to find ways to help children stay aware of their bodies while watching and using screens.

These "energy and concentration" techniques were so successful that I had to spin them off into a specialized workshop. Five years ago, during professional development, teachers started telling me that students of all ages and backgrounds were getting more restless, agitated, and "wiggly." Exceptional learners and students with disabilities often face special physical challenges, but those children were being "mainstreamed" in many schools. At the same time, physical education and recess time and budgets were (and still are) shrinking in school schedules nationwide, leaving kids stranded in their bodies with no outlets for exercise. No wonder there are so many behavioral issues testing teachers' classroom control to the limits.

I believe in mindfulness and meditation training for children and have my own approaches for quieting minds in the classroom. But much of the "acting out" that teachers face can be handled with exercises that function as a simple pressure valve, allowing children to blow off steam. To address those needs, I now teach a seminar called Instant Recess where I share these techniques with pre-K and elementary school teachers. Done in three- to five-minute segments, the exercises give teachers a fast, fun way to improve classroom control, boost student concentration, and augment learning outcomes. Done in thirty-second segments, those same exercises will improve focus and help keep children grounded in their bodies while using screens.

I talked earlier about how the initial priming process engages the child's whole body and mind. That's a very important first step. Once you've taken it and once the child has grown to expect that he will need to use energy and concentration to keep his mind awake while viewing (as well as talk about what he sees), I've provided a broad range of other questions and cues that help children to deepen and enrich the viewing process.

Please bear in mind that I'm not saying you have to do any of this, or that not doing it will damage your child. What I'm offering are some simple techniques and strategies to reframe viewing behavior, and to proactively challenge the prevailing brain chemistry of viewing. Specifically, that means challenging the domination of the lower reptilian brainstem (the limbic system) or the right brain, which is most active when watching screens. As with any technique, it's important that this be used in a way that's balanced. The shake-stop itself is fun and silly. It is also empowering and enormously strengthening for children. The ability to control your own energy and your own mind is very important. In tiny children, those abilities start with actions that are extremely simple and achievable.

Chapter 10

Mindful Viewing

Almost two decades ago, Tenzin Gyatso, the current Dalai Lama wrote, "Film and television, newspapers, books and radio together have an influence over individuals that was unimagined a hundred years ago. This power confers great responsibility on all who work in the media . . . [as well as] each of us who, as individuals, listen and read and watch . . . it is not the case that we have no power over what we take from the media."[1]

His Holiness is not placing blame, just reminding us that we consumers, not just content providers, have important choices and responsibilities in the brave new digital world. It took me more than a decade to work out practical strategies to support twenty-first century learners and their parents in making those choices and meeting those responsibilities. I call it Mindful Viewing and it will someday merit its own book.

Mindful Viewing is a twenty-first century empowerment practice. In my work, it involves engaging technology and media with an awakened mind and body so that we can discern when and how we're being affected and decide what to do about it. I know Mindful

Viewing is completely achievable because I learned it from a four-year-old, who told me, "I get to choose what goes into my mind."

The changes that support Mindful Viewing are small but mighty. Priming our minds with purpose before picking up the screen; noticing how we're responding to games, apps fiction and nonfiction content; checking in with our bodies every hour; making new meaning from our screen experiences by talking about them; paying critical attention to the details within screen-based content; developing critical filters. It's really not hard—we do most of these things all the time! We just don't notice that we're doing them or apply them to screen time.

We need to make these simple changes in how we watch and use screens individually and with our families. And when we do, we'll start growing exponentially because nothing is more powerful than fully activating our human technology . . . before engaging the technology we've created.

Metacognition

Making the distinction between what I'm feeling and what the character is feeling is the start of metacognition—the ability to reflect on our own thoughts. It's a form of higher-order thinking that allows us to understand, analyze, and control our cognitive processes, especially when we're learning. Picture a world where humans lack the ability to understand or analyze their own thoughts and you'll see why it's so important.

However, metacognition is also one of our most vulnerable faculties in the twenty-first century and it is under constant threat and stress from the intentions of the advertising industry. The job of the people creating audiovisual ads is to get you as fast as possible from "see this" to "buy this." I'm not accusing or making a judgment here; it's a simple fact of commercial advertising.

Advertising is designed to collapse the process of reflection, assessment, and decision-making. Those are very crucial, precious faculties, but instead of blaming media-makers and attacking those who create and purchase the commercials (although that's sometimes necessary and effective), it's far better to push back by cultivating our native intelligence and abilities. We can safeguard the potential of our children's minds by helping them to notice and talk about their responses. When they bring what's happening on the screen and in their own minds into fuller awareness, they will begin to question content and to build their own media filters.

When they bring what's happening on the screen and in their own minds into fuller awareness, they will begin to question content and to build their own media filters.

The great news is that if we give our children the chance to reflect regularly on their responses to media, we strengthen them against the predations of advertising in two ways. First, they'll be accustomed to reflecting before they act and thus be less vulnerable to compulsive buying. Second, they'll have the expertise to notice that their responses are triggered by specific parts of the ad that are designed to anchor their attention. Most ads will have characters, settings, colors, music. Some even have plots! There's a lot to talk about using the same approaches I've already presented. Making commercials or ads the topic of screen talk is a brilliant way to activate the cerebral cortex and put some distance between your child and the "buy me that" battle cry of the lower reptilian brainstem.

What Goes Through My Mind When I'm Watching?

Getting a child to exercise the capacity of reflection in regard to any audiovisual text is often revelatory. It's not expected, it's not what most people do, and it is an incredibly powerful developmental step. Children who attended festival screenings were often surprised when I asked them about their thoughts on the movie. For some of them, it was a revelation to learn that they were even having thoughts about the movies. I've mentioned many times that we never show a movie without priming the mental pump, and part of that priming process in the very early days was to ask the question: "What are some of the things that go through your mind while you're watching a movie?"

There is always a wide range of responses. Some children would say, "I like movies when they're funny and when they make me laugh." Or, "I like when I'm reminded of something fun that I've done and when I see it again in a movie, it makes me want to do it again." But there was always, in every screening, a sullen child with his or her arms crossed who answered, "Nothing." That's what I call a "golden" answer even though it often discourages adults by making them think that the dialogue is over before it starts (it isn't), and that child doesn't want to talk to them (he does).

When a child answered, "Nothing," I would just smile and say, "Okay, wait a minute. So you've never laughed at a movie because you thought it was funny? You've never looked at someone on a screen and said, 'Wow, that guy looks just like someone I know!' You never saw something and felt sad because it reminded you of sadness in your own life? That's never happened to you?" By the end of that little litany, the child was always laughing along with me and with his peers. He and the rest of the audience realized that we *all* have thoughts about movies. We just don't usually notice them.

When we're watching audiovisual texts, we are constantly responding and there are hundreds of things that go through our minds. Paying attention to those things allows us monitor our own responses and to keep a healthy distance between ourselves and what we're seeing on the screen. My filmmaker friends sometimes dislike this part of my technique, and I don't blame them because it can be perceived as being at odds with their artistic goals.

Julian Fellowes, the creator of *Downton Abbey,* attended my 2009 festival for a screening of his beautiful film *From Time to Time,* adapted from Lucy M. Boston's *The Chimneys of Green Knowe.*

> When we're watching audio-visual texts, we are constantly responding and there are hundreds of things that go through our minds. Paying attention to those things allows us monitor our own responses and to keep a healthy distance between ourselves and what we're seeing on the screen.

When I was talking to the audience about the importance of voting, I reminded the children, as I always did, to think about what you like, what you don't like, and why. Julian lightly cleared his throat and stepped in at that point, saying, "I would very much prefer that you focus on what you *do* like, if at all possible." He needn't have worried. Featuring Dame Maggie Smith and Hugh Bonneville, later stars of *Downton Abbey,* the film captured audiences' imaginations like none other that year, and it went on to win the prized Best of Fest award.

It is often the purpose of art to transport audiences and offer them insights into themselves and their world. Many filmmakers and other artists reach those pinnacles of achievement and it's our great good fortune to have access to their brilliant work. I'm not proposing that we shut ourselves off from great art, monitoring our every thought and response. Imagine what we'd lose by not allowing ourselves to be available to those experiences!

But the vast majority of screen content does not fall into the category of any kind of art, let alone great art. And because commercial messaging dominates so much screen time, I'm suggesting that by practicing Screen Smart skills and screen talk we'll be better able to recognize those works that deserve fuller access to our deeper selves. But first, we need distance and discernment so we can choose what to let in to our minds. With distance we can activate critical thinking, frame questions, make new meaning, and reflect on the relative credibility of what we've seen. But to start those sophisticated thinking processes and keep them moving, I have to know that what's happening on the screen is not the same as what's happening in my mind.

Throughout this book, I've framed the screen-talk process as an organic offshoot of normal family and parental interactions. I want to add that language I've used in scripts to introduce the physical and intellectual frameworks of Screen Smart skills isn't as important as building a relationship with the child when you're introducing those ideas. It's less important that FBSS are perfectly understood than that it be fun for the child to do the movements of FBSS and then try to apply them. It has to be fun. If it's not fun, mindless viewing and screen addiction will win. Our job as parents is to make co-viewing a movie or TV show or playing a game together as much fun as having a book read aloud.

Generating your own family's standards for viewing and screen engagement is a great start. Then you measure the success of what you're doing with your children by the degree of interest and engagement that they bring to the discussion of what they've watched. Most often, children will swiftly become adept at recounting the stories and the details within those stories. That's why you're there to ask them about what they're thinking and feeling. Before you know it, they'll move on to voluntarily sharing their feelings in ways that build family intimacy.

There are, of course, some children who are going to want to talk about their feelings first because they are extremely sensitive to what they're watching. One way to redirect what you view as an overreaction is to guide them gently toward the "fun" of talking about the details of what they've watched—unless, of course, the details are what upset them. Then take a different tack. You don't have to get them to focus on the details of that part that has upset them or overexcited them. Reference a different part of the film. Ask them, "In what part of the movie or show were you upset?" If the "upset" is too extreme, then redirect by talking about a different show or a different movie that you know they liked. The same way that a child will want to have a beloved storybook read to them over and over again, the child will want to tell you what happened in a part of a movie they loved.

The standards for screen talk will also change as your child learns and grows, just as reading expectations change over time as the child learns to read. You can easily gauge growth in reading by the child's ability to identify the patterns of letters, then the simplest, shortest words, then rhyming words, then more complex words. By continuing to read to the child, gradually adding more mature and challenging books while interacting with her, you'll naturally progress through highly sophisticated reading processes. And that interaction with you, the parent, is one of the greatest stimulators of neural networks, social-emotional intelligence, and whole-brain thinking.

Remember that reading a book to a child is multisensory. Normally you're holding the child, so there's physical contact. There's visual stimulation from looking at the colors and images. There is also aural stimulation from the process of reading and listening. This multisensory web is what we want to replicate during screen time. Even half an hour once a week makes a huge difference.

> This multisensory web is what we want to replicate during screen time. Even half an hour once a week makes a huge difference.

Standards for measuring progress in screen talk would include noticing the child's focus, retention, interest in discussing what they've watched, ability to discuss what they've watched, ability to get deeper in recounting the details and perhaps the inferential reasoning behind what happens in the story, and then moving on to disclosing their feelings and thoughts about the content that they've viewed. Just think of what a rich series of interactions you can have with your child and how frequently that opportunity arises—because your children are viewing and using screens all the time!

Noticing What We Feel When Gaming

It was the beginning of my third session with a large kindergarten class in a school where forty languages were spoken among the student body. I was finishing up with children's answers to the question, "What did you see on a screen or do with a screen that was fun, and why was it fun?"

When I called on Raymond, he said, "I got seven kills in Call of Duty." The five-year-old was trying to smile, but he only succeeded in looking like he felt sick.

I gently leaned forward and asked the boy with a smile on my face, "Wow, that's a lot of kills. How did that make you feel?"

Hesitantly, Raymond responded, *"Gooooood."*

I smiled again, "Really? You don't sound sure, Raymond. Can you tell me what part of getting those kills felt good?"

Big smile, "Playing with my brother."

"Ohhh," I said. At that point, I made eye contact with lots of other kids in the class.

"So it's fun when someone we love is playing *with* us." Children nodded. I continued, "But let's think about this a little. Remember when we talked about the kind of people we want to be? What did we say?" Lots of little hands went up.

Jenna said, "We want to tell good things."

Brianna: "We want to be nice."

Malik: "We don't kick or hit."

Mac: "We want to help people."

I said, "Yes! You remembered so much!"

With an innocent, questioning tone, I asked, "So . . . do I want to be the kind of person who feels happy when other people are killed? Even in a game?"

As children were shaking their heads "no," I made eye contact with Raymond and smiled so he would know he hadn't done anything wrong. I paused for a second and then said, "If we see lots of killing or 'make kills' on screens all the time what can happen?"

Jen: "We can get scared."

Petra: "We think we could get killed."

Isahi: "Maybe we wouldn't care anymore."

I asked, "Is it good to care about people being hurt or killed?" Almost everyone in the class answered, "Yes!"

I responded, "So we have to notice how we feel if we see those things." I paused again and then said, "This is so great! You figured out something important—noticing and talking about how we feel when we watch or play with screens helps us. Not everyone figures this out, not even grown-ups." The children looked delighted at that.

I continued, "I bet that we wouldn't have figured it out unless Raymond had told us about playing Call of Duty with his brother. Thank you, Raymond!"

I quickly went on with the rest of the session, and at its conclusion, Raymond came to me. He said, "Miss Nicole, I don't want to be happy to kill. I'm going to ask my brother to play a different game."

Eager Accountability

Accountability for time spent with screens is most successful when it is integrated into the activities that families normally undertake together. In other words, when it becomes a holistic part of the family culture so that kids talk about what they've watched and they're invited to ask questions about it. It's a two-way street. Parents have the expectation that children will be able to and want to talk about their screen experiences, and children have the expectation that they'll get to talk about what they've seen. As those expectations are met and the screen-talk process is repeated, it becomes natural for parents and children. You'll have layers and layers of experience with making new meaning from what's been seen and with including screen talk in normal family dialogue.

When I watch something knowing that I'm going to be talking about it, the way I watch is completely different, and that's also true for a child. It's a brain booster! But accountability isn't something to be strictly enforced with punitive consequences if the child doesn't perform as expected. On the contrary, developing accountability is as fluid and malleable and enjoyable as any other activity that you undertake with your children.

Just continue practicing that open, inviting tone to encourage children to disclose what they've noticed and what they're thinking and feeling. Accountability for screen content invites children to look into their own minds and gives them the chance to process what they've seen by talking about it. Fun, bad, sad, and scary are aids to accountability and springboards to noticing and discussing details. As you keep talking with children, their ability to reference character and refer to the arc of the story using beginning, middle, and end will naturally increase. When you find them utilizing the more sophisticated vocabulary for FBSS to describe what is happening in the story, you'll hear increasingly mature observations. During any of that process you can ask questions about the social-emotional impact of the viewing experience.

"So how did you feel when Character X fell down the well?"

"How did you feel when the wolf was chasing the pig?"

"Was it scary?"

It's fun because a child will talk about the story, character, or moment of the movie being scary, but that's different than the question of whether or not the child was scared. And so with a two-year-old, you can start (by the third or fourth time that a child has mentioned that something was scary) by asking the question, "Were you scared? I can tell that you're saying the movie was scary, but does that mean that you were scared? Or was the character scared?"

When you ask that question, for the very first time a child may say, "Mommy, I'm not the character! I know that." Some children are very advanced; they already know that, and they may look at you in a way that makes you wonder why you asked the question at all. But that happens very rarely with two-year-olds.

Nell Minow, the Movie Mom, tells this insightful story about children's fears during the film *Bambi*. She went to see *Bambi* with the young child of a friend. They had prepared the child for the scene with the death of Bambi's mother, and she breezed right through that part of the movie. The problem came at the end of the film when Bambi appears as an adult. The child repeated over and over, "That's not Bambi!" and cried torrents of tears. She didn't understand that the image on the screen was Bambi all grown up, and instead thought it was another deer and that Bambi had died just like his mom.

Children are literal. They don't interpret or intuit nuance the way we do as adults. That's why, as we discussed in the beginning of this chapter, it's so important you never assume how your child is responding to something on a screen based only on their external reactions. Unless you talk it out and ask specific questions with caring and compassion, you may not ever know.

> Children are literal. They don't interpret or intuit nuance the way we do as adults.

You're the Boss of Your Device!

I had an exciting opportunity to help balance the introduction of technology for kindergarteners who were "geeking out" in a school where tablets had just been provided. Thirty children were learning to share eight tablets, crowding around tables. When the tablets were turned on, there was a chorus of excited "*Oh's*" and I remember one little boy named Jeffrey saying, "It's like magic!" Right then, I stepped in and asked the teacher if I could say something.

I said, "Let's put the tablets down just for a second. Did you hear Jeffrey? Jeffrey said, 'It's like magic!' That sounds exciting right?" My first words acknowledged Jeffrey's insight. They communicated that I noticed and shared the excitement that Jeffrey had voiced.

"But I want to tell you a secret! Did you know that the real magic is in here?" pointing to my head, then pausing. "You are the real magic. Why? What's up here?" still pointing to my head.

Then I let them tell me that it was their "brain, mind, what's inside your head, what makes us think." There were many different answers. Then I said, pointing to the screen of a tablet I was holding up, "This may look like magic," then I put the screen down, "But the real magic is in here—what's in your mind. Did you know your mind is one-thousand times stronger than a tablet or a computer?"

There was a chorus of "Whoas" and "Wows."

I continued, "What you can do with your mind is the real magic."

"In fact, what happens here *(I pointed to my head)* is every bit as important as what happens here *(I pointed to the screen).*" A lot of little light bulbs went off in a lot of shining minds. I could see children thinking, reflecting on the idea that their own brains could be as powerful as the magical devices that had just been given to them.

Later, when I was back working at that same school, the teacher reported to me that this particular group of children was less "screen obsessed" than classes with which I hadn't spoken.

Of course, what I told the children was neither a fantasy, nor an exaggeration. This experience and the empirical information about the complexity of our own brains were the catalysts for integrating those ideas into Screen Smart skills using a nifty little rubric that I call "Lead or be led." Its goal is to create distance between our children and their digital devices, by making them aware that their "human technology" is the equal of any phone, computer, or tablet. Although I risk getting on a humanist diatribe here, I think it might be worth a short rant, because human beings, fully human beings, are extraordinary. Every one of us is a multidimensional, multiprocessing miracle.[2]

While screens can be extremely useful servants, they make terrible masters. Using this dazzling technology when I am too young to understand that this is a tool, not the coolest toy ever, not a device that completes me, promotes me to others, and is integral to my identity places my humanity at risk. Even if I see the adults in my life spending more time with it than they do with me, this device is just a tool. And I am its master. It is there to serve me. These devices have no rights or purpose outside of service to humanity. That's a fixed point, a *sine qua non*.

But if you're having palpitations because you believe that I've crossed a line and I'm compromising the inalienable rights of your device, you really may need to step down and step away from your screen.

For this tool to be useful, I need to control it and *know* that I control it. I need to know that it is separate from and not "a part of" me or essential to me. The minds that created these remarkable and seemingly magical devices are human. And humans created these tools, to expand our abilities, enhance our capacities, and improve our lives. When we appreciate the processing power and graphics of a new laptop or the upgrade from the iPhone 7 to the iPhone X, a certain amount of gratitude and delight in these enhancements is natural.

However, if we engage digital technology through the lens of the technocratic fiction that it is inherently superior to our own minds, we are confining and condemning human civilization to the paradigm of inferiority. In practical terms, we are voluntarily doing the groundwork for the mega-corporations whose endgames include the commercial hybridization of humanity and technology. Instead of assessing, reflecting on, and then calculating the moral, ethical, and human outcomes of such steps, we appear to be programming ourselves to accept the advances of artificial intelligence (AI) and neural implants as inevitable.

We're told that there will be no sacrifice in the richness of the human experiences and that implanting chips to unlock doors at work is a worthwhile tradeoff for giving our employers access to our whereabouts and activities 24/7. But these, as Harari says, are all stories. Should life's rich sensory banquet be sublimated in favor of boosting computational skills? Should we share our inner lives with chips and processors, making them available to monitors (or hackers) with a few clicks? Does any array of skills—no matter how extraordinary—seem worth the risk of dehumanizing instead of rehumanizing and fully inhabiting our human potential? Let's at least raise, examine, ask, and argue the questions with one another before throwing in the towel of human civilization.

The Risks of Instant Gratification

In the 1990s, long before the advent of the smart phone, teachers were already saying that they felt they "couldn't compete" with screens because children were acclimated to expect "nonstop entertainment" and commercial breaks. Now, with the "pass back" phenomenon, children are watching screens from the age of six to eighteen months. Pass back refers to parents' habit of "passing" their mobile device from the front seat to the back seat of the car to entertain even the littlest ones who don't have their own device. The research isn't in yet and the pass-back generation hasn't yet matured to high school age. But each year, more and more teachers comment that students are profoundly uninterested in education and learning.

While the inadequacies and deficiencies of our current education system have much to do with waning interest in academic success, Walter Mischel's marshmallow experiment with preschool-aged children at Stanford University in the 1960s and 1970s may shed some additional light on children's disinterest in education. Mischel and subsequent researchers showed that the ability to delay gratification was established as one of the most reliable predictors of success in later life.[3]

So before providing very young children with the thrilling experiences and expectations prompted by tablets and screens, it may be a good idea to remember that the design and purpose of these devices is to retain your focus and provide instant gratification. We have a culturally ingrained and commercially reinforced belief that we should be gratified and mesmerized as quickly as possible, and as often as possible, by our screens. That's how really smart software and hardware creators have designed them. By repeatedly handing smart phones to children ages two to seven, we are offering

> By repeatedly handing smart phones to children ages two to seven, we are offering them a formative experience with a device that inculcates expectations of instant gratification when the single biggest predictor of their success as adults is the ability to delay it.

them a formative experience with a device that inculcates expectations of instant gratification, when the single biggest predictor of their
success as adults is the ability to delay it.

Sadly, I'm no longer surprised when preschool and kindergarten
teachers tell me, "We see children at age four so frustrated just trying
to put the square peg into the round hole that they give up."

"If some of my students don't get it right the first time, they get
angry."

"Too many of my students won't read. They just try to swipe the
pages of the book."

But how can we complain about children being easily frustrated
or lacking grit and persistence when we've habituated them to instant
gratification with the swipe of a finger?

Learning to Infer a Larger Meaning

The ability to infer is the launching pad for comprehension, not
only in reading, but in viewing screen content as well. Inferring is the
process of creating a personal and unique meaning from details in the
text. When children draw inferences, they are combining information
from that text with relevant background knowledge to make new
meaning and gain greater understanding.

Inferential reasoning is the ability to look at something on a screen
and posit reasons for the way the creator has constructed that scene,
make predictions, or draw conclusions. It's an important step that
moves from walking to running with a few simple words like plot,
character, and setting. How can you ask a child to infer accurately
and meaningfully if they don't understand the concept of plot? I'm
not saying that they can't infer without knowing the word. I'm saying
that they'll infer faster and better and have richer neural networks
and better storage and retention capability if they're aware of plot and

can sequence their viewing into beginning-middle-end. So knowing character, plot, and setting are foundational to higher-order thinking. They enhance viewing and reading the same way knowing the language of a country helps you unlock the culture. Those words unlock the culture of the story. Naturally your enjoyment will soar if your understanding is activated and continues to be refined. That understanding is predicated on knowing the structures of the story.

When those words are used over and over again, children will learn what they mean through direct experience. During co-viewing, they give you hooks with which you can tease out your child's brilliant observations, helping him to notice details and connect the dots in the story. If you can activate a child's awareness of character, plot, and setting in this way, you also learn more about your child because you'll have a more specific way to engage his interest.

Trust me, just saying, "So, did you like it?" is the great conversation stopper. But asking, "Who was your favorite character?" will always get the child thinking. Remember to pause for the answer and then ask, "Why? Why was that your favorite character?" If you get a shrug, ask some more specific questions, "Did you like what the character did, or said?" If the child says "Yes," ask, "What did you like about that?"

Once you have primed with energy and concentration, and introduced FBSS, character is usually the easiest place to start a dialogue during co-viewing. At this point, it might be a good idea to revisit active listening. If you have genuine curiosity about the child's response rather than parental concern, she will respond to you. Anyone would! Children are like everyone else. If you are asking me a question that is flat simply because you're my parent and you want to check in, I'm not going to want to answer. My reluctance has nothing to do with the question; it's about what asking a flat question says about our relationship. I don't want that relationship with you. When a child refuses to answer a question, they're often refusing an auto-pilot relationship with you. They want something deeper and better.

If you're practicing active listening and you still find that your child is hesitant about responding, this might be a good time to share your own experiences. I recently overheard a parent do this following a festival screening of Weston Woods' *Wolfie the Bunny* based on the book by Ame Dyckman. Her six-year-old son had voted for *Wolfie the Bunny* as his favorite film. But, as I was standing with them, he paused to think when she asked him his favorite part of the film. Then his mother asked, "May I tell you my favorite part?"

She paused to let him answer yes, then continued, "My favorite part was when the bear ran away in the grocery store." Sometimes the child will chime right in with his favorite part and you can ask him why he liked that part. In this case, the child laughed, and his mother did something that we call a "fast redirect." She said, "Help me remember. What was the character that scared the bear? Do you remember what that character was?"

The boy said, giggling, "Oh Mommy, you're so silly, that was a bunny!"

I started laughing with them and asked the boy, "Do you know what the word 'character' means?"

The boy answered, "The people in the movie." To stretch the learning moment, I asked, "Are people the only characters we see in movies and stories? Are there other kinds of characters? In fact, what were the characters in this movie?"

"Bunnies and wolves and bears."

"Yes! What are bunnies and wolves and bears?"

"Animals." More giggling.

"So people can be characters and animals can be characters. Anything else?" Often children will talk about bees, or robots or trolls or toys, but if not, you can prompt them by asking, "What were the characters in *Wall-E* (or *Toy Story* or *The Lego Movie)?*" When they tell you (robots, toys, etc.), "Well, let's call all those kinds of characters *things.*" Now you're ready for your simple definition:

"So characters are the people, *(pause)* the animals, *(pause)* or the things in the story or the movie. Let's say that together!" Then, right there while exiting the theater, I went for a few more questions: "What was your favorite part?"

The boy answered, "I like that the bunny wasn't afraid of the bear." Another girl holding her mother's hand chimed in, "I like that the bunny and the wolf were really a family." Another boy filling out his ballot said, "Everyone felt like they belonged somewhere at the end." That quick confab at the end of the screening was an eye-opener for parents. As one dad wryly commented, "I think you just showed them that learning can be fun."

At home afterward, if you have the time, seeing the child's interest and feeling that this is a great moment for screen talk, you can ask why he liked the bunny and the wolf becoming a family. You may hit social-emotional gold and gain a truly special bonding moment, one that's tied to the dialogue you just had rather than the movie you just saw.

It's worth adding here that Weston Woods was the first company to focus on making movies out of children's books, and their DVDs are available, with study guides, in thousands of libraries and schools.

Integrating character, plot, and setting into screen talk is essential for visual literacy, and in the twenty-first century, visual literacy in early childhood is another cornerstone of future educational success. Luckily, as you've seen, the structures in many games and narrative audiovisual texts align perfectly with the stories in books, and our

> Both solo viewing and co-viewing afford natural opportunities to leverage literacy skills and higher-order thinking.

kids are already watching "screen stories" every day. Both solo viewing and co-viewing afford natural opportunities to leverage literacy
skills and higher-order thinking. The big change: stop segregating
screen experiences and start including them in the natural scope of
topics that we discuss with our children.

Chapter 11

Short Films That Encourage Discussion

I'd like to give you a couple of examples of films that lend themselves brilliantly to emotional intelligence, disclosure, and self-awareness. Because I've spent a lot of time on the pause and question (P&Q) approach, here I'm going to focus on the kind of discussion you can have with a child at the end of a short film that they've seen all the way through.

Meatballs and Catching Anger

The Swedish Meatballs is a series of eight-minute, nonverbal, animated films by a Swedish filmmaker, Johan Hagelbäck. Two of the most affective and powerful of those films are *Meatballs and Catching Anger*, and *The Meatballs and Sorry Bullies*.

In *Catching Anger*, we first see a happy family of meatballs. The dad meatball has a job at a macaroni factory. His boss gets annoyed after a book falls on his head, and he sends red arrows of anger into the daddy meatball. You see the daddy meatball get red, and red arrows start coming out of him. His whole face changes, including his teeth. When this movie is played for children ages two to eight, you can hear a pin drop. Every child has experienced anger, and they've experienced anger from parents. What this movie does is to draw that experience out and make it very safe. (Although I have to add, that out of a thousand children who saw this film, two covered their eyes or needed lap time during the film.)

Over the course of the movie, daddy meatball goes home and makes mommy meatball angry because we can "catch" anger from each other. When his parents get angry, the little boy meatball gets angry. Then when his friend tries to play with him, he loses his patience and starts pounding on a ball. Red arrows are coming out of him, so she goes away. She goes home, and who's there but the boss meatball. So she makes the boss meatball feel better simply by "rubbing his owie" and blowing on it. And when she blows on it, she's sending "happy thoughts," which is what the children said when we asked them. The happy thoughts take the form of little yellow stars—very few of them, no big special effects—and there's a very light sound as in a tiny bell ringing. Because the boss meatball transforms on screen, you can see that the child's gentle, laughing approach has stripped him of his anger. He goes back to work, and his employee, daddy meatball, is still angry. Then, the boss meatball does for daddy meatball what his child did for him. Then daddy meatball goes home and does the same—he sends happy thoughts to each person who was angry.

At the end, you can start an effective discussion about anger with some very simple questions. Although I'm presenting those questions in the order in which I use them most frequently, you can use them in any sequence that works well with your child.

"So this movie showed us what happens when people 'catch' anger from each other. Have you ever seen someone get angry?" (All children have seen anger and it's almost always made them uncomfortable.)

"How did you feel when the other person got angry?" (Just let your child explore that moment. Maybe it made her nervous, maybe she got angry, maybe she got scared; all answers are okay.)

"What did you do?" (Again, it's possible your child did nothing, and that's fine. This isn't an interrogation, it's a bonding and sharing experience. If your child isn't forthcoming or is hesitating, it might help to share an experience that you had getting angry. One mother in a parent workshop told the group that sharing a story about learning to control her temper changed her entire relationship with her son. Then she reconnected the screen talk back to the movie.)

"So how did you feel when you saw the characters on the screen getting angry?" or "What did you think when you saw the characters on the screen getting angry?" "Have you ever 'caught' anger from a friend or a brother or a sister?"

Some children will admit they've gotten angry when a peer or sibling was angry; some will talk about being scared or worried when their *parents or caretakers* got angry even though you've asked about friends. (If the child just shrugs or disconnects, it's good to cast the net for other emotions.)

"No? How about a bad mood? Have you ever 'caught' a bad mood? Or what about when someone you care about is really sad?" (Let the child respond.)

Although children saw "meatballs catching anger," by continuing the open-ended questions, you're encouraging them to make what teachers call "text-to-self" connections that help with retention and with behavioral modification.

As the dialogue unfolds, most children gain a powerful two-part realization:

First, they start to consciously recognize that their emotions can be affected by others, and that their emotions affect others.

Second, the child recognizes that she can choose how to respond and how to be affected.

"Has anybody been angry at you and made you angry?" Yes . . . that has happened a lot.

"Have you ever been angry at someone?" Every child has been angry.

"Why did you get angry?" or "What happened to make you angry?" Let the child share the details.

Here's how to gently guide them toward the realization that they have choices:

"We have a choice when people send out anger, don't we? We could get angry, too, but in the movie did the little girl meatball get angry? *(Pause for response.)* No? What did she do instead?"

Children tell me, "She was nice," "She wanted to help," "She made him feel not angry," "She sent him good energy."

"So we know that we can catch anger, and we know we can send anger to other people, right?" Always, after each gentle question you pause. If no child responds, you gently press ahead: "So we have a choice! What choice do we have? If we don't want to catch anger or send anger what could we do, what could we send?"

Children will usually start thinking about all the positive things they could send, but don't worry if your child doesn't. You can lead the witness with a smile: "You could send something . . . positive. What could *you* send?"

Here are some things children have told me:

"I sent love to my friend when she was sick and she said it made her heart warm."

"I sent 'feel better' when my sister was crying. She said it was like a hug."

"I can send a happy feeling without talking and it helps my mom."

You can gently prompt the child, "I bet you can tell me about one time when you sent a positive feeling, a good feeling to someone else." And if your child still doesn't respond, just table it. It's another moment for ELMO, enough, let's move on. But don't dump the topic or give up. Just use a statement like, "Okay, we can talk about this some other time."

And now that you've heard some of the positive feelings and ideas your child can send, you can guide him toward future actions and behaviors.

"What would we *want* to do when somebody is angry? What would our choice be? Could we make that choice? How often could we make that choice?"

Here, we get to talk about choices, but at the same time, underlying the whole process is the understanding that people get angry and it's okay. It's not the end of the world when someone gets angry at you or when you get angry. It doesn't mean that nobody will ever love you again. It doesn't mean that your family doesn't love you or that they're bad people. It means that, in that moment, they made a choice to send anger. And maybe we or they would want to make a different choice next time. Maybe we can help someone who's angry make a different choice, and maybe we could help ourselves, too.

Viktor Frankl addressed this so elegantly in his book *Man's Search for Meaning*: "Between stimulus and response, there is a space. In that space is our power to choose our response. In our response lies our growth and our freedom."

> "Between stimulus and response, there is a space. In that space is our power to choose our response. In our response lies our growth and our freedom."

As adults, we often struggle with the issue of choosing our responses. Imagine the gift you would be giving your child if you could convey this and practice it just by watching a seven-minute video together.

The Meatballs and Sorry Bullies

The bullying film, *Sorry Bullies*, is a fresh and simple story about the same little girl meatball who sends happy thoughts in *Catching Anger*. On the playground three boy meatballs, who are friends of hers, tease her and take her hair bow. You can tell that one of the little boy meatballs is an unwilling participant in the bullying. He doesn't really want to do it. But the boy who isn't a willing participant doesn't stop the other two. After crying, the little girl leaves and the three boy bullies are left thinking about what they've done. That night, the boy who didn't want to participate in the bullying can't stop thinking about what happened. In his mind, he sees the girl crying, so he gets up, retrieves the bow from where he's hidden it, and, in the middle of a rainstorm, he gets his two buddies. All three of them go over to the little girl's house. When she comes to the door, they all step back as if they're afraid that she's going to yell at them, but she doesn't. She welcomes them in and all of them are able to play with a huge box of bows.

What children have said when we interviewed them at the end of the program is that seeing someone bully someone else in an animated form helped them because it made it seem less catastrophic. When a child feels threatened for the very first time, or mocked, or cut out of his or her group, it's a precipice moment. It can be terrifying for different children. Some children pass through it very quickly, but for others, it's formative in an extremely impactful and hurtful way. To see bullying on screen that shows the feelings on all sides in a setting that is at once playful, specific, and abstract at the same time, allows children to channel their emotions and become less fearful of how they would get over it if it happened to them. It also helps them realize what they did experience maybe wasn't as scary as they thought it was. It puts them in a different relationship to the experiences that they've had.

After I showed both Meatballs movies at Disney School, a three-year-old boy named Lee came to talk to me before the class started. Lee said, "A bully pushed me down."

And I said, "Oh, no, Lee, what did you do?"

He said, "I cry, and I was 'cared" (He couldn't say the S sound at the time.)

I asked him, "Did you tell anyone?"

And he said, "No."

I asked him why, and he said, "The boy say no tell."

I said, "Well, what do you think would happen if you told someone?"

Lee said, "He hurt me more."

I asked, "So what did you do?"

And he said, "I stop cry and say sorry. And when I say sorry, he go. And I feel better."

I was really surprised, and I asked, "Lee, the boy hurt *you*, so why did *you* say sorry?"

Lee responded, "I don't want to bully. If I say sorry, I can't catch to be a bully."

That was really profound for such a young child. We had talked a lot in his class about how the boys who took the little girl's bow were sorry for what they had done. And during the first film, we had talked about how we could "catch" anger, the way people "catch" a cold.

What Lee did was brilliant—he connected the dots between the two lessons. Instead of insisting that the person who was mean to him should say "I'm sorry," he said it to be nice, and to defuse the danger that he might become a bully himself. It was an amazingly mature emotional choice, and in this instance, it yielded a good outcome on the playground.

Lee's example shows that children who see something on a screen that is emotionally supportive about a disturbing experience are able to absorb strategies and try them even when they are experiencing stress. But Lee's application of those strategies far surpassed what I had anticipated for social-emotional learning outcomes from the Screen Smart program.

Dip Dap Scary Thing

When children seem to be "unreasonably" terrified by something they've seen on a screen or in real life, I have sometimes used the short film *Dip Dap Scary Thing* in a therapeutic context as a means of helping children cultivate their own awareness and recognition of their overreaction. In *Dip Dap*, a little humanoid creature is trying to befriend a very nervous little ghost. Poor Dip Dap tries to engage the ghost in activities that would be fun for both of them, but what ensues is a comedy of errors where Dip Dap continues to terrify this ghost by accident.

One-on-one, it's possible to lead a child into an understanding of the ways that any of us can become uncomfortably frightened. When children see the ghost being terrified of these very simple things, they laugh. And through that laughter, they vent and expel some of their own fears.

There was a hypersensitive child in one of our kindergarten classes. She would become upset during every film that had a slight increase in volume or loud noise. She was not autistic or an exceptional learner—she was extremely sensitive and extremely smart. Sitting down with Bella after watching this movie was a fascinating process because this time she didn't put her hands over her ears and drop her head to the floor during the film, despite its many loud noises. Instead, she was watching and laughing.

I asked "Bella, did you like this movie?"

Bella said, "Yeah, I liked it." She was not overly enthusiastic, she just said she enjoyed it.

I said, "I noticed that you weren't worried about how loud it was and you didn't have any problem with the ghost screaming when he got scared."

And she said, "Well the ghost is kind of like me."

I said, "How is the ghost like you?"

"People are always trying to make me feel better and they're always doing things that make me feel worse."

"So why would you like a movie like that?"

"Because it means I'm not the only one."

"And because you're not the only one, did that make it easier for you to watch it and listen to these loud noises?"

Bella said, "Actually, I didn't notice the loud noises and I didn't notice the loud screaming. It just felt like me."

Chapter 12

Emotional
Intelligence

The emotional messages coming from screens can be complex, and often, like the *Bambi* story, a child's reaction to a particular scene in a film or a streaming video isn't what it appears. A parent may casually observe their child laughing and assume the content to be innocuous or enjoyable, but that laughter may be a sign of fear or nervousness, not amusement. What you see isn't always what you get with children, especially when they're watching screens. In this chapter, we'll explore emotional intelligence and screen time, explaining why learning how to ask the right questions and really *listening* to the answers is vital. You'll learn how to help a child recognize what they're feeling during screen time, how to identify those feelings, and how to talk about them so that screen time can strengthen the child's emotional intelligence, identity, and self-confidence. This chapter is about how to utilize screen time to help children become more aware of their emotions and to learn how to navigate them.

Early childhood experts from Jean Piaget onward talk about the child's natural narcissism. That narcissism manifests in small children as selfishness partly because their needs are so great. Lacking the capability to provide for themselves, they depend on adults for their very lives. Unfortunately, narcissism unchecked becomes toxic, and we can see that in children's lack of ability to identify or empathize with the emotions of others.[1] The skill of noticing, perceiving, and relating to people's feelings is also called emotional intelligence, or EI. The more research is done, the more we see how important this particular human faculty is for our children's success.[2]

At one high-achieving private school in Chicago, the third- through eighth-grade teachers specified a schoolwide need that astonished us. One teacher put it most succinctly. She said, "My students don't even know that other children have feelings. They're in their own personal bubbles and think they are the only people that have feelings."

That not only surprised us, but it meant that we had to change the entire premise of the program and shift it to address those needs. So in every screening, we would tease out greater awareness of the characters' feelings and then complement that by encouraging disclosures of the students' feelings *about* the feelings that the characters were having. What this did was ensure that students repeatedly heard from their peers about the feelings they had and wished to discuss.

Hearing that whole grade levels of students lacked empathy and the ability to recognize feelings in others was as motivating for me as hearing from pediatricians a decade earlier that parents weren't talking to their children. Following the workshop I taught for the Illinois Chapter of the American Academy of Pediatrics, I spoke to many doctors who intimated that not only were dialogues about media not taking place, but parental interactions with children were limited to directives and check-ins but didn't extend to conversation. We can fix that! Seriously.

Social-Emotional Learning

I think that our emotional patterning depends, in great measure, on the relationships we have with those closest to us in our earliest years. If those relationships don't include active dialogue in which heartfelt disclosures are supported by equally heartfelt responses, it can be hard for children to find their footing with social-emotional learning. The best and strongest social-emotional learning (SEL) starts at home. Ideally, it begins long before children start to watch screens.

Social-emotional learning isn't a skill to use as a Band-Aid or even a quick fix for times when your child is upset by screen content. Quick fixes may be useful, but strong SEL and interrelational skills are the result of a support structure of ongoing relationships and positive habits of communication in the family. To encourage the skill of confiding feelings, one first has to encourage the skill of noticing feelings. And not all children notice their feelings, let alone notice the feelings of others. So step number one is: "What am I feeling?"

> To encourage the skill of confiding feelings, one first has to encourage the skill of noticing feelings.

You can help a child connect to his feelings simply by asking him what he's feeling. Naturally, you don't want to overshadow your child's emotions by making them too subject to disclosure. There are things that everybody wants to keep private, and no one wants to have all of their feelings dissected and discussed. So keep it in balance. If every emotion is the subject of endless comments and questions, any child will start to feel frustrated and possibly criticized. That said, parents sometimes need help identifying the best times and opportunities for social-emotional interaction. Happily, there are "hooks" in everyday life to help ease out such disclosures.

Another good place to start is by observing the emotions of others. Media and screen content of all kinds afford a strong springboard for noticing the responses of characters, then differentiating and refining our own awareness of how we are responding. Co-viewing gives parents a rich opportunity to develop this "emotional feedback loop" while, at the same time, neutralizing the danger of children becoming inured to the feelings of others. Imagine missing the chance to lay the foundations for empathy simply because we never talked about the feelings of characters or the feelings that we're having.

Talking to Your Child About Screen Emotions

When purposely engaging your child about the emotional content he's viewing, a lot depends on the media text that you select and how you set up the discussion. It's better to use media content that does not talk down to the child and leaves room for the child's own imaginative response, rather than filling the auditory and visual space with eye and ear candy that is common in a lot of commercial media. If you are watching a program where characters exaggerate and telegraph their emotions in ways that make them and their feelings look foolish, that's a poor choice. Understated, authentic expressions of child-centered concerns offer very rich ground in a very short period of time for inviting crucial awareness of what the characters are feeling.

Here, I'll give an example of a screen talk that held many more challenges than you'll normally encounter in talking with your child. I was asked to speak with a group of three- and four-year-olds at a preschool where parents had been fighting among themselves and tensions in the school were running high. I picked a five-minute episode from the Danish Little Tot series that I had programmed at the BAMkids Film Festival in Brooklyn. In this film, *Little Tot, Eating Jam* the main character is a pinky finger who's tired of being small. Little

Tot had made friends with an ant and invited the ant for lunch, but he knew his mother didn't like ants.

After priming, and starting the film, question number one is always very simple: "What do you think the character is feeling?"

One child initially responded, "He's sad."

"Did he say he's sad or does he just look sad?"

Another child said, "He looks sad because he's alone and his friend isn't there."

"Is he *just* sad? Or is there something else he's feeling?" I let them think about it, and then asked, "Do you know the word *worry*? What was the word Little Tot used?" A little chorus of voices, "Worry!"

"Yes, Little Tot said he was 'worried!' What does 'worry' mean?" At this point, I needed to be prepared to tell the children what "worry" was, in a simple way. "Worrying is when I think that something that isn't good might happen. It hasn't happened yet, but I'm thinking about it. So do you remember what Little Tot said he was worried about?"

If the child doesn't remember, show the segment again, cuing them with a lighthearted, supportive voice. "Let's watch that again and see if we can figure it out!"

We watched again, and the children started talking right away.

"He's worried about what his mommy might say to his friend."

"He's worried if she would be mean to his ant friend."

"If your mommy isn't nice to your friend, he won't like you."

This gave me the chance to help children make the text-to-self connection with a simple comment. "Wow, everybody might be worried about those kinds of things, right?"

Once the child has identified the key point, what the character is really worried about, then it's possible to introduce the question, "Have *you* ever been worried about something like that?" That day, the children and I had a deep discussion about how hard it was to be friends with someone when your parents and their parents didn't like each other. They talked about "being nice anyway" and how they could be friends at school but not at home. Teachers later told me that the children were less stressed about the hostilities because they *knew that the problems weren't their fault.* That's a lot of mileage for a little screen talk.

It's a very tender and enlightening process. When you're encouraging this kind of disclosure from a child, you need to be prepared to go wherever the child feels like taking that discussion. If you can be flexible, you'll gain your child's trust in ways that can strengthen your relationship with her over a lifetime.

Once, I was asked to use screen talk to help a family that was stressed by a new joint-custody arrangement. Again, I picked the short film featuring Little Tot. The child answered "yes" when I asked if he'd ever been worried that his mommy or daddy wouldn't like someone he liked. He turned to his mother and said, "Yes, I'm always worried about what you think about Daddy." That moment helped both parents see how their stress was affecting their son, and he started sharing other feelings that led to lots of hugging and reassurance. "Your mommy will always be your mommy and your daddy will always be your daddy. Even if we aren't together, we'll always love you."

When you create a safe space for the child to communicate his feelings, he will often start sharing things that are so meaningful and so important that you can potentially save him years of struggle and sadness in the future. A child who has the courage to say that he's concerned about how you'll respond about Grandma or Daddy or any other person in his life is often taking a risk, not making an accusation. He's asking for you to accept his feelings and saying that he has picked up on signals that you may not know you've been giving. Calmly allowing this kind of communication while remaining attentive to your child's needs allows you to build honesty and trust in ways that will double the strength of your family's social-emotional network.

Let's look at some other ways to handle that kind of dialogue at home. If you co-view a program where parents disapprove of a character's friend, you could ask the question, "Have you ever been worried that I wouldn't like someone that you like?"

If your child says, "I'm scared you could yell at me when my friends are here," don't get upset. And don't make promises that you can't keep. The most important thing for you, the listener, parent, or caregiver, is to stay centered and relax instead of getting defensive. This magical moment of disclosure can be ruined if you say, "I don't do that! I've never said that your father can't come here. I've never said your friends aren't welcome!"

Remind yourself that you're talking with a child and what you're doing is fostering emotional resilience. As I said, it takes courage for a child to disclose a feeling that may make their primary caregiver uncomfortable. So the first and best response to a disclosure like that would be to thank the child for telling you that.

"Oh, I'm so glad you told me that, sweetie."

Your priority is to support and *get authentic feedback from your child.* Set aside guilt as well, or you'll start making excuses to the child instead of leaving that disclosure right there on the table and celebrating it. You don't have to do anything about that feeling! A feeling is a feeling. It deserves to be appreciated and noticed for its own sake. You notice it and move on. If the child seems upset when making this kind of disclosure, then it's appropriate or beneficial to gently ask additional questions. Again, those questions can't come from defensiveness or guilt. Rather, they need to come from genuine compassion, curiosity, and caring.

If the child is upset when telling you something like "Yes, I worry about you not liking this person," a good question would be, "Oh, do you know why you would be worried about that?" If the child doesn't know, that's okay. You can also frame that question as, "Would you like to tell me why you're worried about that?" Then you can ask in a caring, compassionate way, "Have I done something or said something that made you worry?"

The most important thing is to let the child's emotion or feelings have pride of place rather than being obscured by *your* feelings, which could very easily overset or imprint on the child's feelings.

Probing, Not Pushing

Let's take another example, perhaps one that's fraught with fewer emotional perils. A simple strategy in watching any well-constructed media is to stop it and say, "What do you think the character is feeling right now?" Get an answer. If the answer is overly simple and you think the child has the capacity to go a little bit deeper, you can ask in a positive, encouraging, nonjudgmental way, "What other words could we use to describe how that character is feeling? We said 'sad' that last time. What's another word? Is the character just sad or could the character be *gloomy*? Let's say that together!"

"*Glooooomy.*" (I usually make a sad face while saying the word.)

And then it becomes a game! But the child will remember the process of identifying feelings and get used to noticing that kind of information on screens. If the child knows that the parent is alert to that kind of content, the child will want to emulate the parent's awareness. That's the upside of early childhood imitation.

To assist the child in recognizing and identifying their own emotional reactions, we only need to ask the question, "Has that ever happened to you?" Or, "Has that ever happened to someone you know?" Then ask, "What about that feeling? Is that a feeling that you've felt?"

There are many ways to frame a question so that the child doesn't feel interrogated. Sometimes setting a two-question rhythm like the one above will help because it's less threatening. Of course, if you ask the question with too much intensity, then it intrudes on the privacy of the child's emotions. Tone, rhythm, and especially eye contact and encouragement will make that dialogue go smoothly.

Building emotional vocabulary is the same process, effectively, as building any other kind of vocabulary. You use the word and the child may ask you what it means or simply understand what it means based on the context. When I'm teaching

> Building emotional vocabulary is the same process, effectively, as building any other kind of vocabulary.

social-emotional learning as part of our Screen Smart programs, I'll go through a whole list of words and it becomes fun: "Let's find more words to describe these feelings!"

That's a perfectly good exercise to do with your child at home, but I also think that uncovering feelings can occur more naturally over time during co-viewing. Although vocabulary building can help "tease out" emotional intelligence, your child's ongoing awareness of emotions that are conveyed by characters, music, or dramatic action comes first.

When he was ten years old, my godson Alex visited my office to talk about being on the Children's Jury for the Chicago International Children's Film Festival. I told him that he'd want to think about whether or not he wanted to be on the jury because he would probably have to see one hundred movies and he'd have to keep all of those movies separate in his mind and vote on them to pick the ones that should be awarded prizes. He paused for a moment and he said, "Tante, why do people cry at movies?"

And I said, "What a great question! Why do you think people cry at movies?"

He was quiet for a moment and then he said, "Because they can't hear the things that are in their own hearts."

So I asked him, "So what does that mean to you? What would it mean if you can't hear something in your own heart?"

He said, "They have a feeling, but they're so busy looking and listening to other things that they don't recognize it."

I asked him if he thought it was because people were distracted, "Do you think people are just too distracted to see these other things?"

Alex said, "No, I also think it can hurt to look at those things and they don't want to be hurt."

"You asked me why people cry at movies. So if they don't want to be hurt, how do they end up crying?"

"Because they went too long without knowing what they're feeling." This was a truly perceptive insight for a ten-year-old, and I told Alex that I was proud of the way he looked at his own feelings and those of other people during our talk.

As caregivers, parents, and teachers, we can open up those moments by listening rather than by answering. Active listening is often our best tool in helping children identify and notice the depth of their emotions. Of course, it's good to remember that nonverbal communication plays a huge part in the success of interactions that are driven by likes and dislikes. So coming down to the child's level, making eye contact, keeping a pleasant expression, and staying relaxed will also support your success.

> It's good to remember that nonverbal communication plays a huge part in the success of interactions that are driven by likes and dislikes.

Engage the child by being truly accepting of what they volunteer and disclose, and ask genuinely respectful and interested questions.

Then actively listen to the answers. It seems very simple, but if you think about the way we often relate to children, the priorities of getting them to school and appointments on time or purchasing items they need so often take precedence over real intimacy. Of course, I don't recommend that you take the time for this kind of full exploration or disclosure when a child is having a meltdown in the checkout line at the grocery store. Just understand that the meltdown itself may provide a path to dialogue after it has been detoxified.

The short-term strategies that you use in the moment to calm or quiet your child are a separate issue altogether. They are behavioral and relate to self-regulation rather than to SEL. Social-emotional learning can only take place in an environment of mutual trust, support, and genuine interest. Unfortunately, the intensity of a meltdown obviates the possibility of having any meaningful discussion at that moment. Like weathering a storm, you have to stay centered and let it pass.

Empathy Leads to Success in Life

Empathy is crucial for success in every part of life and that success is threatened when SEL is stunted.[3] Noticing what other people are feeling and how they are responding to us is the basis of friendship, love, persuasion, teamwork, and interactions with those who teach us and transform us. Being comfortable with our own emotions also means being more accepting of ourselves. When we're accepting of ourselves, we are far less likely to respond defensively and interact with people on the basis of perceived threats. People who are unfamiliar with their own emotions

> Noticing what other people are feeling and how they are responding to us is the basis of friendship, love, persuasion, teamwork, and interactions with those who teach us and transform us.

and the emotions of others operate in every social environment on the basis of perceived threats. They are constantly in or struggling with fight-or-flight mode, which is intensely stressful and demeaning. Feelings of low personal worth and humiliation can then lead to the temptations of lying and manipulation. An entire group of unwanted behaviors is ready to take over the mind of someone who is not aware of their own emotions and the responses of others.

By contrast, caring about the emotions of others and what happens to them creates empathy that strengthens family, community, and personal connections. Setting aside the obvious desire of every parent to avoid having their child become a sociopath, the danger of toxic narcissism looms for any child who has not noticed that what he or she does can hurt others. Yet when you present a clear instance of bullying to a child by screening a short film, you will observe high levels of empathy and understanding from children who, minutes before, were screaming for their friend's bag of popcorn.

The Toboggan

Recently, at a screening for the Elliott Donnelley Youth Center in Chicago, I showed a three-minute film from Canada called *The Toboggan*, after asking children to pay attention to what they were feeling and thinking during the movie. The premise of the film, directed by Richard B. Pierre, was extremely simple: a child of color, clearly a newcomer to the snowy wastes of Canada, is attempting to use a garbage bag as a sled to have some fun on a winter day. He's accosted by bullies, who mock his sled and his clothing, and this interaction is observed by a little girl on top of the hill. Without saying anything to this child about the interaction that she saw before, she offers him a ride on her sled and says that her father has okayed it. So she's done two things: she's saved him the humiliation of reliving the earlier interaction, and she's called on a higher power, the parent, to induce him to accept something that he otherwise might refuse. And in fact, in the film, he refuses it at first.

The children in this audience live in an economically challenged neighborhood, but instead of the anticipated, "Man, I'd beat those guys up! I would never let that happen to me," the children surprised us. In written comments they talked about the insecurity of going to a new place and hoping for acceptance, and the disappointment of being rejected. During the post-screening discussion, they talked about the danger of "becoming a bully when someone bullies you" and how "hard it is not to shut down."

The children see the main character humiliated in the first thirty seconds of the film, but as the three-minute movie progresses, instead of shutting down and becoming a bully himself, they notice that the character allowed himself to trust again and be reached. He had the strength to open himself up when the young girl offered him her sled. At first he didn't want to accept it. When we ask kids why he wouldn't want to, they say, "Well maybe she was just fooling around. Maybe she would laugh at him." Kids automatically saw all the dangers of accepting a gift right after being put down. But the triumph of joy was in the child's face as he went down the hill on the sled, then dragged it back up to return it to the girl. At that point, the girl offers another level of validation by asking him, "Do you want to do doubles?"

When screening the same film for formerly homeless young mothers at Austin's New Moms, Inc., facility, I asked, "Why would she ask him to do doubles at that point?" They responded without hesitation.

"She stopped just thinking about him and started thinking about them."

"She realized she could make a new friend if she could get him to hang around."

"She went from doing something nice for someone else to wanting some fun for herself."

Instead of divorcing himself from human interaction and compassion after being pushed down, the main character showed strength first by accepting a gift, and then by trusting the girl enough to make an active connection that would be ongoing. Kids get it. Because they were primed for viewing and asked to be aware of their feelings, they remained emotionally available to the film's many messages. This emotional availability allowed them to see the injustice, feel and identify personal and social relevance, and talk about it honestly with their peers.

In three minutes, a film can prompt an amazingly complex, layered set of feelings, responses, and interactions that proceed along a profoundly human arc from disappointment, humiliation, and self-rejection into hope, joy, and connection. When every step of that journey is tracked with interest and empathy by children, we've given them a chance to affirm their own humanity.

Chapter 13

Increasing the Sphere of Interaction Around Screen Time

Throughout this book, we've focused on the sphere of adult-child interactions and looked at ways to enrich those interactions. Facing our digital future with our humanity intact means broadening the family sphere to include screen time. As well, we'll want to include other family members, friends, and caretakers who may participate in screen time with our children.

Inside this new and positive sphere of adult-child interactions, we're interacting differently around and with our digital devices. We're noticing new things on the screens, in ourselves, and in one another. We're developing new neural networks, developing new trust and new pathways of communication between parent and child, and we're leveraging the time they (and hopefully we) spend with screens to improve learning, communication, and empathy. You don't need to create a master plan for using screen time to improve your children's lives. If you use the strategies we've been discussing, their lives and learning will be enhanced.

After you create and inhabit the first sphere, you can invite others into it, which is the best way to acclimate them. By inviting others into the Screen Smart sphere, and letting them experience priming, focus, and dialogue, you're transferring and sharing vital knowledge. Many parents have started Screen Smart play groups with children as young as three years old. After a couple of sessions, the children start to lead the groups themselves.

In addition to teaching healthy screen habits and improving the quality of family and child communication, you can also help the child transfer her energy out of viewing and into applied creative activities. Much of what I've described has focused on dialogue and the development of higher-order thinking skills. But these techniques also lead quite naturally to a broad range of hands-on arts activities.

Drawing. After several sessions of co-viewing, instead of talking about what your child thinks about what she saw, ask her to draw her favorite scene with her favorite character from a program she recently saw. You can do this every few days with different programs or movies, and get the child to describe what she's drawn and why that's her favorite part. Another great exercise is to draw the same character in a different setting or with different clothes. Or to draw a different ending for that show or movie. (Kids often think they can improve on the ending of something they've seen and they're usually right!)

Modeling clay or PlayDoh. Make a character or an object from a show you really enjoyed.

Origami. If there was a bird or flower in a movie that your child really liked, it can be fun to try making one.

Lego bricks or blocks. Build structures from the setting of a movie.

Cooking. If the characters enjoyed a food or meal that really looked wonderful, why not try making it!

Pretending or acting. If a character has a special adventure, the way Amran does when her camel gets sick in the Ragdoll Foundation movie, *Amran's Film, Ethiopia*, it can be fun to pretend that we have a camel and now we have to find a "camel doctor."

Make a short movie with your phone or tablet! There are at least ten good, short "how to make a movie with your phone" tutorials online. Just do a quick search.

Record your young media critic. If you don't want to start with filmmaking, it can be fun and illuminating to record a child's "review" of a film, a show, a game, or even a commercial. Just prime, have a little dialogue using some of the questions I provided earlier and record the child talking about what she likes, doesn't like, and why. It's a great confidence builder and if you save these short videos, the child will be able to see how her skills grow over time.

Of course, most of these activities can be done without using digital devices as a springboard. Using media as a point of departure for creative exploration won't make your child derivative as an artist. You're not buying the whole indoor mini-movie set, lunchbox, backpack, dolls, and costumes for *Frozen*. You're just using the screen experience to help them channel creative energy out of viewing and into hands-on, creative activities.

Sharing Screen Smart Skills
with Caregivers

Before you hire any babysitter, you'll want to spend fifteen minutes walking him or her through the Screen Smart process. I've trained nannies and other caregivers very quickly, by moving through the priming, P&Q, and screen-talk process with them in the role of the child. You're inviting them into this new sphere of interaction and making sure they know how special it is. After sharing your "when and how much" guidelines, you say to the caregiver, "Instead of just picking a program and letting Harry watch by himself, I'll want you to watch with him. Co-viewing, watching together, and talking is the way we handle screen time when we're watching shows or when we're starting to play a game. And we make it especially interactive. There are three steps. One, we prime with energy and concentration, and share a viewing goal. Two, we watch and we talk about the program in real time or pause to ask questions. Three, after the screening, we can keep talking or do art activities based on what we've seen. You need to ask questions and listen to her answer about special details she noticed. Or you can talk about what she liked, what she didn't like, and why." I'm always careful to add that discussion shouldn't be forced, so if it's not playful or fun, and if the child isn't enjoying it, move on to the next activity.

A quick aside: when children have demonstrated strong focus and communicated well during screen talk, it's a good idea to encourage them. Hearing, "Wow, you did such a good job noticing those details!" is empowering and exciting for your little digital natives. I'm guessing that you would praise your child if you noticed that she was reading with increased fluency or asking you questions that impressed you with her depth of reasoning. Naturally, you would acknowledge her achievement and compliment her. Give that same kind of positive feedback during or after screen talk, too. Learning and using Screen Smart skills engages numerous developmental domains. It is a highly sophisticated, intellectual, physical, and emotional activity that merits real recognition, especially in early childhood when such recognition is formative.

If your in-laws or parents frequently take care of your children, then invite them into this improved parent-child sphere of interaction. That invitation is done in the exact same way I outlined above. Even better, they may have the chance to participate with you and your children in co-viewing at home. With close family members or even the parents of your child's friends, they can often go along and be part of the fun. Set the time limitations (when and how much), suggest the content, and keep the basics of being Screen Smart close at hand. Those basics are outlined in Chapter 14.

If you have older children who babysit or share screen time with your young child, here are a few basic guidelines that give everyone a way to participate:

1) **To older siblings say, "We're** going to do this a little differently from when you were younger. We're going to be talking about games and shows and movies while we're watching."

2) Once your little ones gain confidence in Screen Smart skills, let them *teach* their older siblings, something I also outline in Chapter 14. They can show their sibs the energy and concentration exercise, teach them about FBSS, and share insights during P&Q.

3) When in doubt, skew collective program choices younger. As your older children are included in screen talk and co-viewing, they'll be more open and supportive of your "younger and more sensitive viewers." I've known families where older kids started to confide in the younger ones,

saying, "Yeah, now I agree with Mom about the scary stuff. It does kinda get stuck in your mind."

As you learn and share the screen-talk process with others, you'll have some successes, some failures, and some surprises. Don't force the issue and don't give up. Just keep talking with your own children and their friends. I've met many parents and grandparents who are naturals and who quickly leverage time with digital devices to talk with their children. Trust me, they're not all filmmakers or early childhood experts. One screen-time savant worked in a company that provided employment resources for ex-offenders and drug users. Miss Katie had an extremely tough communication style and a no-nonsense approach to her job. But during a casual conversation about my work with screens and early childhood education, she truly lit up, describing the way she watched shows on tablets with her grandson and the kinds of questions she asked during screen time. "It goes way beyond babysitting," she said. "We talk about so many details that his kindergarten teacher says he's ahead of his class."

Beware the Adult-Free Zone!

In the absence of communication and interaction, children's time with screens can become an adult-free zone by default. This gives them a deceptive and potentially dangerous feeling of autonomy in a world that they are not equipped to navigate. Sure, adults see the dangers of disturbing content, but we often respond with simple directives: "Watch this, don't watch that." Then the child is on his own. But children aren't the only ones adversely affected by unlimited screen time, are they? In the last ten years, we've been through a fascinating cultural cycle similar to what might happen if a child suddenly had unlimited purchasing power in a candy store. They binge. They get sick. Sound familiar?

Mastering Your Own Screen Time

Ten years ago, many parents' biggest complaint about their kids was that they wouldn't put down their phones or their tablets for face-to-face talks. Today, according to Sherry Turkle, PhD, children are often the ones begging their parents to put down their phones to talk to them![1] On the surface, it shows that adults are so entrenched in their own unbalanced ways of engaging screens that they are providing role models for children that will lead to additional unhealthy screen attachment.

If we're going to use these extraordinarily powerful digital resources to our best advantage and lead full, authentic, human lives, we need to start noticing how we're being affected. We need to talk

> Mastering technology isn't about improving our tech skills. Mastering technology means mastering ourselves.

about how we're responding to what we view and make beneficial changes. Mastering technology isn't about improving our tech skills. Mastering technology means mastering ourselves. We pick up screens when we need them, when they serve a purpose, and put them down when we've finished what we were doing. Can you do that?

One millennial mom said, "I check my Facebook feed one hundred times a day or more and feel like I have to answer every tweet from every friend. I'm an extrovert, but it's even too much for me. I don't want all my friends contacting me at once. But that's what happens. There's no control over the volume of content and it feels like my life is being washed away."

When I asked her why she felt she had to read everything, she said, "I don't want to be too old-school, we've all got to keep up." No, you don't have to keep up. You really don't. It's not old school to cherish your free time and safeguard your peace of mind. We have the strength and the awareness to reserve our precious time for things that nurture and complement our lives. As adults, we recognize the "mechanics of engagement" used by advertisers, game designers, news outlets, and movie directors to attract eyeballs. But even when we feel pressured to participate in screen time as a cultural experience, or "keeping up" with friends, or being on the cutting edge, we really know that none of that is true. We're simply acting as if it's true and the market that counts every *click* profits from our actions.

> The demands for our participation in screen culture become louder, shriller, more intrusive, more disturbing as the drive for profits grows.

The demands for our participation in screen culture become louder, shriller, more intrusive, more disturbing as the drive for profits grows. That's not a political statement, it's a simple fact. Content providers want to make money. Not a problem, we all need money. But it's not your responsibility to give it to them. Your will to resist digital seduction is a thousand times stronger than the temptations of a tiny electronic device. Including Internet kittens.

The bonus in freeing ourselves from the tyranny of our digital devices is that our children will notice. So if we use screens in healthy, productive ways, there's a good chance they will, too. For children, healthy screen use includes active communication with adults. The great hall of storytelling contains thousands of doors to dialogues with your children and you entered that hall the first time you read a book aloud to a child. So if you've been reading books with your children, you already know how to do this! Just start applying your bedtime story skills to co-viewing when you watch screens together.

Do We Overprotect
Our Children?

When it comes to early childhood, a lot of parents have told me that because they're concerned or nervous about the dangers surrounding their children, they focus generally on "protecting, instructing, and controlling." Are those dangers as overwhelming as we seem to believe? Statistics show that child abductions and murders and abuse have fallen, but our sensitization and concerns have grown exponentially. Few would argue that those fears are not inflamed by the fiction and nonfiction we consume.

I had the chance to chat with several parents on Chicago's Northwest Side after they practiced healthy screen habits for a couple of months.

"It felt so great to find balance and stop the cycle of fear-driven control-parenting."

"All we needed to do was start talking. We also learned to step back and observe the things we were seeing on screens, not just respond emotionally."

"Watching with my four-year-old, I started to notice my own feelings and responses. It changed my choices! No one had to tell me. I just didn't like the way those programs made me feel."

As you'll see healthy screen habits reach far beyond screen time.

"When we moms would talk before, we'd jump right to complaining about things. Maybe because we had uncomfortable feelings we didn't want to share? So we just complained about the things that made us uncomfortable. It was like a big old pity party before. Now all the moms are really communicating and sharing. Ideas, questions, disagreements—it's all okay. We're better at talking with each other so we're better at talking with our kids."

Parental Controls on Devices

Some parents have asked, "Wouldn't it just be easier to use parental controls?" Absolutely. But it's a thousand times less effective, in part because kids are clever about getting around parental controls. Let's consider the technological fail-safe mechanisms that have been developed to solve the problems of too much screen time or exposure to inappropriate content. From the V-chip, to the parental controls on the Internet, to numerous apps that track your child's screen experiences and alert you, you've got a lot of choices. Having filters in place and preventing your children from wandering into sleazy Internet neighborhoods is a great idea *combined with* screen talk and Screen Smart skills.

In fact, there are many apps that you may find useful in monitoring your child's viewing. A few that I recommend include:

The Xooloo apps, which are designed for both the management of adults and children's screen time: Xooloo App Kids, Xooloo Digital Coach, Xooloo Parents.

Screen Time, which restricts time spent on several different apps or websites. It even allows you to create a checklist with rewards for things you want your children to complete.

Net Nanny, which takes care of usage on both phones and computers, with alerts, time management, and chosen blockage of programs.

But the benefits of *talking* with your kids about their experiences and discovering what they really think and feel is still paramount. In fact, sharing your own online experiences with your children can be an effective way of bonding with them while peeking quickly at the dangers lurking behind random clicks. Unfortunately, the drive for parental control over screen time has totally overshadowed the need for discussion. Let's change that. Even if you master all the parental control technologies, get tracking apps that alert you if your child is watching inappropriate content, memorize the criteria for content provided by Common Sense Media, and limit screen exposure to homes where you know parents share your views of appropriate content, after all that, you've just provided the best possible media prison, and nominated yourself as warden. You've established as much parental control as you can.

But that sole strategy precludes the child from developing his or her own filters, judgments, opinions, and ways of managing their media experiences. Developing Screen Smart skills is a wonderful, messy process, and kids really need to learn to do it for themselves: sorting through and organizing their experiences with screens, venting about them, confiding what they like and don't like, and processing and making meaning from content by talking about it. The crucial developmental steps that help children build healthy relationships to screens are skipped if we focus only on controlling screen time.

> The crucial developmental steps that help children build healthy relationships to screens are skipped if we focus only on controlling screen time.

That said, I still recommend ad blockers for any digital device, service, or app you let your child use. There are only so many times you can say, "No. Because I'm the mom and what I say goes."

Sharing Personal Stories with Your Kids

Between helicopter parenting and parenting-as-a-friend, some of the strict adult-child boundaries dissipated—but not always in good ways. Let's consider personal disclosure again. It can be stabilizing and very comforting for a child when you briefly share a personal experience that parallels theirs. It's a way of bonding and showing your child, "That happened to Mommy, too." This kind of sharing can (but doesn't always) alleviate a child's fear, disappointment, or concern. You simplify, share, and step back, letting your child draw her own conclusions. If it helps, great. If it doesn't, move on.

However, it's quite another thing to talk about your experiences with few filters the way we do with our close friends. If our emotions, self-doubts, and self-recrimination are in full voice, that kind of highly charged disclosure tends to overwhelm and crowd out whatever your child was trying to talk about, replacing the child's experience with your own. No wonder she won't clean her room! You're using her as your therapist!

So if you notice that it's hard to stop when you're talking about your past with your children, and you're "confessing" rather than sharing, you're on the wrong track. Real sharing involves pausing and listening for your children's responses and then weaving their experiences back into the conversation. But even if you've erred on the side of overdisclosing from time to time, don't close the door to dialogue. Sparing, well-timed confidences can give the child a window into his parent's world and make him feel trusted. Just don't use them to erase and replace the child's own experiences or convince him of anything.

Whole Child Parenting

Children need structure, and they thrive on knowing that there are boundaries and even consequences. Many of those structures in families were eroded by the parent-as-friend movement that followed the baby boomer generation. Then there were a series of new waves in parenting, from the Tiger Mom approach, driving children toward excellence with discipline and goal-setting, to the "everybody gets a medal" model that was intended to curb disappointment and reframe the paradigm of winners and losers. Of course, we can't leave out the ultra-helicopter approach that curiously requires parents to mediate every major life experience, often without input from the child. All of these approaches have been well-intentioned, and each has arisen for a reason, usually to avoid or change something deemed nonbeneficial within the parenting culture.

Let's expand on those good intentions to consider the whole child. Today that means charting and sharing the evolution of their lives in the digital world. Children are whole human beings, and we can help them integrate screens and technology into their lives with enormous benefits if we make just a few changes for them and for ourselves. But those benefits will never be gained without authentic dialogue, community, and expressing our thoughts and feeling about screen experiences. There has to be a place in our culture for those things to be shared outside of a list of responses to a YouTube video or a tweet. Before they wander into the broad thoroughfares of the Internet where they're vulnerable to trolls, before they drown in their friends' Facebook posts, before they're snared by fan sites that simply leverage fandom as a market, they need to learn how to express themselves with their families and peers face-to-face.

We can rehumanize screen experiences by using Screen Smart skills to start talking with our kids, building the foundation for the success of our entire culture moving forward.

More Benefits of Adult/Child Conversation

Although I'm advocating for a richer, evolving, and ongoing form of parental communication with children, please understand that those dialogues don't need to be constant. They just need to happen often enough in early childhood so that by the time your

nine-year-old gets to a dinner table with adults who are having interesting conversations, he can listen and participate and ask questions.
Your children don't need an IQ of 160 to do this. They simply need to
not be ignored, shut down, or excluded. On the plus side, they need
to have that experience of asking questions, being asked questions,
having their opinions listened to, having their ideas and opinions
examined, and having their feelings about their experiences respected
and cherished as the trusting disclosures they are. Even, and sometimes especially, children who demonstrate the classic tendencies of
introverts will benefit from two-way conversation with adults because
those talks will build a body of experience with self-expression that
leads to greater confidence in communicating. When that child gets
older he can favor his preference for introversion or participate in
dialogue with others as he chooses. It's his choice, rather than a result
of insecurity or lack of ability and experience.

Just as important, a child who has practice and experience with live
dialogue where the feelings of others are taken into account will have
better social skills in person and online. We often hear that today's
youth are so "screen bound" that they flounder in "real-life" social and
professional situations. We can save our children years of awkward-
ness and insecurity by talking with them now, so they appreciate good
conversation and understand the dynamics of face-to-face discourse.
It adds another proficiency to their communications toolkit.

Although many tweens and teens are adept at adapting to the
ever-changing dynamics of digital discourse among their peer group,
they still face unexpected challenges, missteps, and bullying. Being
able to hold an actual conversation gives them two advantages in
those situations. One, they'll have a better chance at "talking it out"
and mending fences or ending the communication with dignity and
balance. Two, they'll be more likely to share their struggles and seek
the help they need.

Chapter 14

Lessons Learned

The majority of what's been presented so far focuses on providing very young children with an orientation to screens and digital devices, some of the most powerful influences in their lives. A book-based orientation is the best place to start, as I described in Chapter 8, where the child sits on your lap and you talk to her about what she will be experiencing when the screen goes on. After that orientation, you move into a priming technique that encourages children to use higher-order thinking skills when they are using the devices as well as communicating their screen-time experiences.

I've emphasized that what happens before, during, and after screen use is an important part of building family dialogue around screens, and changing focus and family culture around screens in ways that support children developmentally. Screen time can be used to close the 30-million-word gap just as effectively as books. But ingrained habits of viewing and screen use need to be examined and shifted before that's possible.

The end goal in giving children the tools to express their opinions, preferences, and responses to content is that they will develop

> The end goal in giving children the tools to express their opinions, preferences, and responses to content is that they will develop their own filters and the ability to self-select programs, games, apps, and movies that are positive and appropriate for them to view and use.

their own filters and the ability to self-select programs, games, apps, and movies that are positive and appropriate for them to view and use. Those selections will change over time—you can count on it. But helping children develop those evolving choices is not just empowering, it also takes tremendous pressure off parents to monitor children's screen experiences outside the home because the floodgates of their feedback are open and coming to you!

When children are Screen Smart, they can better regulate themselves and their own viewing. They begin to insist on healthier ways of engaging screens themselves. That's a very special turning point, one that you cannot predict and cannot force. It generally happens when other children in their peer group or their siblings have been invited into this fun, engaging Screen Smart sphere. Being able to identify and share your own thoughts and feelings about the games you play and the programs or movies you're watching is a big motivator.

Through screen talk—the process of acclimating children to priming the mental pump, noticing details, pausing and questioning, talking about, then wrapping up and discussing things that haven't been covered yet—the habit of engaging screens in healthy ways becomes something that they voluntarily want to do.

In schools where children in the Screen Smart program also played together, parents who observed and monitored those play-groups reported that when children decided to watch or play with screens, they would do the mental priming exercise and then talk about what they had watched. Children did this so frequently that while they were playing and doing other things, they would still be talking about the movies they had watched together. That's traction at a level we wouldn't ordinarily expect from an experience that takes place for only half an hour once a week! The secret behind that success? I had started sending home "fun work" with children, giving parents guidelines to practice screen talk at home. Now we know that if parents practice screen talk half an hour once a week, their outcomes will be even better than ours!

Two years ago, at the end of the Screen Smart program, a four-year-old boy came running out of his kindergarten classroom to talk to me when the bell rang. He looked up at me and said, "Miss Nicole, I want to be you for my little brother. I want to teach him to be Screen Smart." Although I was touched and delighted, I also realized how many opportunities I'd missed. I could have been empowering children to invite others into their Screen Smart experiences for the past four years!

In other schools, teachers told me that when students who had been in the Screen Smart program were stuck watching a feature film instead of being allowed to go to recess, those children would get up and teach other children the priming exercises.

Now, in week eight, as children take ownership of being Screen Smart, I offer them a gentle challenge and a chance to lead others. First, I ask if they feel confident in their Screen Smart skills and we take a minute to review those skills.

Being Screen Smart means that when we use screens, we:

- ❖ Use our energy and concentration to keep our minds awake
- ❖ Notice details (FBSS, plot-character-setting, main idea, problem-solution) in the stories or games or shows we're watching
- ❖ Pay attention to what we're feeling and thinking
- ❖ Notice what we like, what we don't like, and why
- ❖ Talk about what we've noticed

After the review I ask, "Do you think you could teach your friends or your brothers and sisters to be Screen Smart?"

Most children raise their hands excitedly right away and I'll often hear, "I've been teaching my sister (or mother or grandma) already!" At that point, I set up a "pair and share" exercise. One child in the pair pretends she doesn't know how to be Screen Smart, while the other teaches her the priming exercises. Then they switch! By the end of the class, everyone wants to go home and share with at least one family member or friend.

> Children love to share expertise. But even more, they love noticing and knowing when they're improving at something.

Children love to share expertise. But even more, they love noticing and knowing when they're improving at something. That's one of the reasons why games and apps are so popular. You know when you're getting better at them! Unfortunately, in our current education system, the measures for growth and improvement are in the hands of systems or adult authorities who are too far removed from children to make their growth feel real and meaningful.

By contrast, Screen Smart and Mindful Viewing are child-centered approaches. They're structured to empower the child so that he notices, controls, and reinforces his skills supported by you, the parent. Children can tell when they are getting better at the shake-stop. They can tell when they are getting better at talking about the characters, plot, and setting, and they get excited about the fact that they can notice their own growth and improvement. It's a very rare experience in childhood and children need the kind of encouragement that feels authentic and earned.

Although I may not earn any friends with this next statement, I think there were and still are fundamental problems with the "everybody gets a prize for participating" approach to competition. First, the approach fails to take into account whether or not the child tried and devalues the efforts of those who did. Participation, like virtue, may be its own reward, but if we award equal value to half-hearted and full-on participation, it's going to be hard to measure growth and even harder to motivate. Second, it doesn't allow children to experience and overcome disappointment, which frequently occurs in life. Third, it doesn't allow them to process all of the rich thoughts and feelings they might have from trying really hard without succeeding. It's wonderful to try hard and not win because you could get better next time!

Don't get me wrong. I'm all for making process more important than product in early childhood, and for calming the cultural obsession with winning. But giving every child a prize isn't the way to achieve that. Letting the competition take a natural course so that someone *wins* through effort or talent and then talking with your child is better, in my view, than giving every child a prize, which creates an expectation of a reward for no effort.

Using the Screen Smart techniques, the child will notice, feel, and express his delight over his success and growth in using these techniques. That self-perceived improvement affords the child a vital new level of ownership over his success and mastery of these skills. Because he knows he's responsible for his own growth, when he experiences obstacles, he'll want to try harder get past them. Because he knows he has control over these skills, he may want to share them with others. Because he knows he's choosing what gets into his mind, he'll be an independent thinker.

Reflecting on Consequences

This brings us to an important component in quelling problems of "acting out" and behaving badly in early childhood. There is no positive place in our culture or personal experience for reflection on the consequences of our actions. Let's be honest. Most people hate talking or even thinking about consequences in relation to themselves. Why? Because consequences mean you've done something "wrong" or "bad." But that's not really true. Sometimes, you've just done something illogical or careless or selfish and you resent the consequences imposed by those actions. So let's just take a cleansing breath and a big step back and realize that consequences are your friends, and your child's friends. Consequences teach you and provide invaluable life lessons.

As parents we can be potent advocates to bring our children's attitudes and experiences with consequences into balance. Of course, some consequences are harsher and harder to bear than others, and our first impulse is to protect our children from them. But with the right communication, those consequences can and should lead to positive change.

If I say to you, "Well, what do you think the consequences of your actions should be?" in a castigating tone, I'm already punishing you by turning an opportunity for real reflection into rhetorical question infused with blame. That's very different from sitting with a child and asking, "What made you think that action was okay?" If you can set aside anger, outrage, and the inner voices telling you you're a terrible parent, you can be curious and caring and compassionate toward everyone involved in the incident—without letting the child off the hook.

Just remember: the discussion is separate from the consequences. You can create an opening within that dialogue that allows the child to tell you honestly what led him or her to that action. We all want to avoid false apologies, fake contrition, and contrived promises of change, right? Those are the unsatisfactory, second-class outcomes we get from forced, inauthentic discussions with our children about disturbing behaviors. On the other hand, when our children trust us, they'll start sharing thoughts they may not have known they had, and start realizing new things about themselves. Authentic discussions reinforce positive ideas and bring up a lot of ideas that children may be censoring or that may later drive destructive behaviors unconsciously. If you don't feel you can manage this kind of discussion, no worries. There's nothing wrong with turning to qualified social workers and psychologists to open the doors to communication.

Healthy Screen Habits:
Not Just Kid Stuff!

Several friends of mine are parents who have recently stopped smoking. Some of them allow their children to verify they've quit in very playful ways. My friend Jeff, who's a contractor, said that when he announced he was quitting smoking, his two-year-old daughter Dottie asked to smell his breath and clothing every time he came in from work because she can smell the smoke. She loves dogs and she pretends she is a puppy. They call it "snuffling for smoke." The "snuffling for smoke" game is valuable in so many ways. It makes children part of the solution and gives them a positive stake in an outcome they care about: their parents' health. These parents stopped smoking for themselves and their families because they wanted to be healthy and see their children grow up. They also recognized how much their children cared about their succeeding in quitting and found ways to include them. But this "child-inclusive" parenting style seems to be threatened by the ways adults and children use their screens.

In her 2011 book, *Alone Together*, Massachusetts Institute of Technology social psychologist Sherry Turkle, PhD, talks about the ways that screen use, including texting culture and social networks, is changing how people relate to society, their parents, and friends. Interviewed by the American Psychological Association's (APA) online magazine, *APA Monitor*, Turkle said, "Children say they try to make eye contact with their parents and are frustrated because their parents are looking down at their smart phones when they come out of school or after-school activities." Remember when parents were complaining that their children's focus was hardwired to their screens? Looks like the pot has just met the kettle. In view of the encroaching presence of our digital devices, it seems that practicing and modeling healthy screen habits is one of the most important things you can do as a parent in the twenty-first century. So what are healthy screen habits and how do we develop them?

Forming Healthy Screen Habits

Developing positive habits starts with the confidence of knowing that you can form those habits and a body of beliefs that inspire you to take the steps toward change. Here are some of the principles and steps that I share with adults who are interested in developing good screen hygiene. Even if you've been wielding a smart phone like a light saber since they first came on the market, these tips can give you a greater power: ending the domination of digital devices in your life.

1) **Preparation.**

What we do *before* picking up the screen matters, and even a whisper of positive awareness and priming can make a difference. This can be as simple as the energy and concentration rubric we use with children (a single shake-stop and softly saying, "mind awake" takes less than five seconds), or as personal as a moment of mindfulness. If you are facing big challenges in your screen work that day, clear your mind, think of a great success you've had, and put a smile on your face to boost your endorphins. Or try one of the "power poses" that social psychologist and author Amy Cuddy mentions in her TED Talk just before you sit down at your computer.

2) **Purpose.**

Be purposeful and know your intention for screen use whether the use is for entertainment, for research, for fulfilling your job responsibilities, or finding a new one. Knowing what you want to accomplish during screen time helps you set limits and structures that will forestall the tendency to be drawn endlessly from screen to screen. For example: write a proposal, write an e-mail, play a game, be entertained.

3) **Mindfulness.**

Stay self-aware during screen use. From time to time check in with your mind and your body. Pay attention to what's going through your mind and how you're feeling. My greatest weapon against screen addiction and screen exhaustion is my awareness that I am being affected, and my attention to noticing how I'm being affected. With this awareness, I can take steps if I am uncomfortable, overwhelmed, or overstimulated.

4) **Time and Timing.**

By paying attention to how you're being affected, you'll learn how long you should use, play, or view screens. You'll set your limits for work, play, or entertainment, and you'll find the best intervals during the day and evening to call on those limits. There are apps that allow you to schedule notifications. Use them! We all need these little reminders.

Self-Support Strategies

Select a set of strategies that you can use for "digital detox" routines throughout the day. When I have numerous converging deadlines on back-to-back, twelve-hour days, I use one of my support strategies every ninety minutes. If my eyes are sensitive or I can feel the stress starting to build up, I use one or more of these seven strategies hourly. We only get one body, so it makes sense to take care of it if we want it flourish. Whatever your work interval, try some of these and build a better list for yourself.

> **Move.** If you've been sitting or reclining too long, get up. Walk around, swinging your arms. Bounce up and down lightly on the balls of your feet, letting your arms and wrists relax and bounce with you. Run up the stairs. Take a short walk outside. Stretch. Swim. Get on your bike. Do five minutes of yoga or any exercise you enjoy. You'll be amazed at how getting your body moving and your heart rate going improves your productivity and protects your body. Recent research not only supports the brain-based benefits of exercise, it clearly outlines the health threats from remaining seated and sedentary for long periods of time.

> **Go screen-free for three minutes.** Once an hour, look at something green and growing. Houseplants, trees, your lawn or garden are all good. Do some deep breathing. If you don't have time for a walk, stand in the doorway and try the HeartMath exercise of breathing slowly "into" your heart (see HeartMath .org). Even thirty seconds can help you release stress.

> **Hydrate.** By all means start your day with your caffeine of choice, but over the long haul of screen time, water is a better friend than caffeine. According to my favorite feng shui teacher, if you drink hot water, it's like giving your organs a bath. Try it with a little lemon or lime.

> **Music.** I have friends who have classical music on all day and others who thrive on heavy metal. Some people listen to natural sounds like streams running, or subliminal messaging. Binaural and isochronic tones are part of brain-wave science,

and can be energizing or they can put you to sleep. Experiment! Test and see what works for you. If some sounds or music make you jittery, those aren't the ones for you no matter how many of your friends love them.

Olfactory reset. Remember how you felt when you were walking along the street and you smelled fresh bread from a bakery, or got a delicious whiff of chocolate from a candy factory? Your sense of smell is the only sense that travels directly to the frontal lobe or forebrain. But if we often need to escape a patchwork of unpleasant street odors, or feel assaulted by perfumes, fabric softener, or bad breath in your office, smelling can be a sense that many of us avoid or block out. Although research on the therapeutic use of different smells may be thin, olfactory stimulation can be enormously helpful for relaxation, stress relief, and a feeling of well-being. I love having different scents available during the day, so I keep essential oils handy. Rubbing a bit of pure peppermint oil on your neck or burning some sandalwood incense can be a great reset button, a moment of mini-recreation.

One screen at a time. Young parents and college and high school students often ask, "How many screens is it healthy to use at one time?" The best answer is *one*. (Yes, I know you can have multiple windows open, but try to avoid the "attention grabbers" that might derail your purpose and monopolize your time.)

Communicate. Hey, it's not just for kids! Talking about our responses to what we see on screens helps us process that information and often makes us aware of thoughts just outside the edges of our awareness. We become more self-aware and, even better, escape unrelieved screen time by interacting with real human beings.

Daily Screen Hygiene

Let's start at the beginning of the day. Do you have morning rituals or have these slowly been co-opted by reaching for your phone or tablet the minute you get out of bed? If you've managed to preserve and reserve part of your morning for self-nurturing, you're on the right track. You're priming yourself for your day and every second is valuable. Getting up fifteen minutes early to meditate, or exercising for thirty minutes, or getting out into nature and letting it fill your senses are all great strategies for bringing your day into balance before it starts. You're sending yourself a message that you matter, and it's a message that will stay with you throughout the day. So whatever your job or schedule or responsibilities, don't pick up the screen before spending a little time on self-care.

When it comes to family breakfast, stick to the rule of "No screens at mealtime!" even if the meal is only ten minutes long. It's still ten minutes of connection with your kids and it will help you keep your (and their) day on track. If you use technology continuously as part of your job, or at home during the day, revisit the segment called "Forming Healthy Screen Habits."

Screen-Free Dining

Let's look at dinner, briefly. Although it can be fun to eat together while watching a movie, in general, gaming or working on screens while you eat is going to impede your digestion. It's going to put stress on your liver and your gallbladder. If you don't believe me, talk to your local acupuncturist or naturopath. More important, screen use of any kind will make you unavailable for family time during dinner. Dinner as family time is one the great bonding engines for family relationships. Don't buy into all those movie and TV scenes of frazzled parents sniping at each other while their children fling food. Spending time with people you love, talking about your day prompts the kind of reflection that gives you insights into your own life. You'll start noticing things in the day that have slipped past you, that should have commanded more attention, or that bothered you and were ignored in the moment so that you could focus on other things. In the middle of dinner conversation, memories of your day arise again, gain your attention, and elevate your awareness. The single most powerful agent of change and self-control is simply you, reflecting on your life.

> The single most powerful agent of change and self-control is simply you, reflecting on your life.

Again, this is called metacognition, the ability to reflect on our own thoughts, and it's one of our most precious faculties. It is also the bullseye on the target of our marketing-driven culture.

Escaping the Pull of the Digital Market

The job of effective advertising and marketing is to build brand loyalty, generate repeat purchases, and move us as quickly as possible from stimulus to response, or in Pavlovian terms, to move us as quickly as possible from "ding" to drool. Advertising is even more influential now that we can be stalked by online ads based on our clicks and searches. Justin Rosenstein, the creator of Facebook's "Like" button, is one of a growing group of high-level Silicon Valley ex-patriates who are concerned that the so-called attention economy conforms more and more to the demands of advertising. As a practiced consumer, you're supposed to move quickly from "I see that" to "I want that." But I'm not sure that we really recognize and accept our complicity in the rise of the "market culture." More important, we have power that we haven't identified and aren't using. So let's think

for a moment. Do I think of myself as a person or a product consumer? Am I able to make a distinction between those two identities?
Do I recognize my right and my power to abstain from participating
in the market?

I appreciate the variety of products available to me. I'm grateful for
the access to abundant information that allows me to evaluate those
products. In balance, it's all good. But just as nonprofit professionals
experience "mission creep," millions of us who are "digital workers"
experience "screen creep." As adults, we're all responsible for the tacit
cultural acceptance of the idea that it's okay, even desirable, for us to
be marketed to 24/7. I'm not advocating for extremist anti-capitalist
activities here, just asserting that it's possible to diminish, with dignity, the strength of the pull of the market, its apps and social media,
on our minds. As Monte Stettin, a brilliant serial entrepreneur in the
entertainment and media industry put it, "Just don't lend them your
neurons."

Most young children don't understand ads and commercials
unless we take the time to talk to them about it. And, remember, they
follow our lead, so if we're dazzled by ads, they'll be interested, too.

What We Say Matters Less
Than What They See

When beginning to speak to very young children about media,
their limited literacy and language skills may pose a challenge. So
when we're introducing very young children to screens, the question
is not just what we say but what we do. As parents, we first need to
look at ourselves and consider the messages behind our actions. How
we respond to screen content, what we do while watching or holding
screens, how we interact with others when we're working on a computer is going to speak volumes to a child. Children imitate us. They

want to do what we're doing. And when they get their own screens, they'll do what they saw us do.

Parents in my workshops often talk about how it affected them when they realized that their children were reflecting their own screen habits back to them. After a parent workshop at the Oak Park Library outside Chicago, one father said, "My baby, she watched me work on my computer, and my phone when she was real little. Sometimes I get impatient and yell at the screen. Now I notice she yells at her own tablet and her teacher says she does that at school and it bothers the other kids. We gotta change that and talk about it."

The mother of a four-year-old said, "Whenever Jeni came up to me while I was working, I'd put my hand up like a stop sign. I visited her classroom on a day when children were learning to use a tablet. A little boy wanted to join Jeni's learning group and I saw her use the same motion I had used when I was in my office. She cut him off completely. I can see that talking about the time I need would have been a better choice."

When it comes to content, we have to keep in mind that when children are preverbal, memories are not encoded in the cerebral cortex—they're encoded in the body. This is one of the best reasons to avoid screen time for children who can't talk, even approved programs. You're not a Luddite. You're not handicapping your child by not having her practice coding for toddlers. You're simply protecting the healthy development of your child's neural networks and vocabulary by prioritizing real, human interactions over virtual ones.[1]

The Parent Who Works at Home
All Day . . . on the Computer

Naturally, if you work from home on your computer, your children will see you staring at a screen for hours. I'm not saying they should never see you on your computer, but closing the door or using a privacy screen while you work can offer many benefits. Not only are you improving your privacy and focus, you're making sure your preverbal child doesn't "imprint" the image of you sitting in front of a screen for hours and hours too deeply. Let's not activate those pesky mirror neurons in our children, and let's be mindful that screen use by others, even when seen peripherally, can trigger our own impulse to do the same.

Later, when the child is able to speak, you can talk about why you are on that computer or phone. You talk about what you do with each screen, making it clear that you distinguish between the screens and use them for very specific things. You're not excusing, you're not rationalizing, you're sharing. This gives your child an understanding that structures are in place.

You're not using the computer because you prefer work to spending time with your children. You're using the computer so that you can spend time playing or talking with them later, after work. Will they fully understand? Probably not. And you'll have to repeat the message more than once. But here's the bottom line: if you don't want to be the pattern card for screen addiction, your child needs to learn that she's not less important than your screen time and you don't prefer the screen to her, a conclusion that many children draw if we scowl while trying to preserve our own screen time.

Over the Labor Day holiday one year, I had to complete a major eighteen-page proposal with seven attachments. So after three generations of us arrived at my mother's lake house in Wisconsin, I told everyone that I would have to meet a special deadline. I apologized and said that I was going to limit my work to those hours when we weren't doing something together as a family, and I added that I was committed to family time so if they didn't think they were getting that from me, they should let me know. This made such an impact on my niece that she stopped what she was doing on social media and waited until later in the evening to reach out to her friends. I, as an adult, was confiding in them, not drawing a line in the sand that said "Keep out." That kind of communication takes young people into the inner circle, validates them, and says that I see them as mature individuals whose time I value. It shows that I value and include them in my thoughts and actions.

The Myth of Multitasking or Multiscreening

The screen choices that we make when we're relaxing after dinner contribute to the way we feel the next day. I've walked into homes for "screen detox coaching" and found adults and older youth using four screens at once. If I've got my tablet, my computer, my phone, and my television on with different software with three screens, I'm draining my mental batteries far faster than I can replenish them with a single night's sleep. If you have Spotify and Facebook up while texting, and you're watching YouTube videos while glancing up at Netflix running in the background, you're living in a four-ring digital circus, and you're going to feel stressed.

This might be a good time to revisit the study on multitasking, done in 2009 by a professor at Stanford University, Clifford Nass, with students from MIT. Students claimed, before the study, that using multiple screens and software simultaneously gave them an edge—they felt they were more creative, more insightful, worked faster, worked better. In the 2010 PBS Frontline documentary *Digital Nation*, producer and mom Rachel Dretzin talked with Nass about the study and its outcomes:

RACHEL DRETZIN: Nass allowed us to film one of his studies, conducted on a group of carefully chosen students.

Prof. CLIFFORD NASS: On a college campus, most kids are doing two things at once, maybe three things at once. These are kids who are doing five, six or more things at once all the time.

RACHEL DRETZIN: The experiment looks simple: identify numbers as odd or even, letters as vowels or consonants. But it's rife with traps in the form of distractions. Nass is testing how quickly these kids can switch between tasks without losing their focus.

Prof. CLIFFORD NASS: Virtually all multitaskers think they are brilliant at multitasking. And one of the big discoveries is, You know what? You're really lousy at it! It turns out multitaskers are terrible at every aspect of multitasking. They get distracted constantly. Their memory is very disorganized. Recent work we've done suggests they're worse at analytic reasoning. We worry that it may be creating people who are unable to think well and clearly.

RACHEL DRETZIN: When I got back to New York, I noticed how much I, too, fell prey to distractions. I kept catching myself in the act, checking my e-mail when I should have been writing a script, Googling something to satisfy a random curiosity. This is affecting all of us.

The full transcript is still available online through PBS and the documentary itself is worth seeing.

Multiscreening does not make you smarter. It's a drain on the brain. If you're listening to music, why are you watching a movie? What's the point? Different parts of your brain are active when you listen to music—this gives you balance and access to a really exciting part of your brain. If you overengage your brain and nervous system by listening to Taylor Swift and playing Words with Friends while watching *Peaky Blinders*, you're creating static between your neural networks and your enjoyment of each media will diminish. Our brains are phenomenal organs, capable of extraordinary accomplishments. But they don't come with surge protectors and being mindful of that fact will serve us well in the long digital future we're facing.

> Multiscreening does not make you smarter. It's a drain on the brain.

Enough Is Enough—
Knowing When to Stop

At the end of the day, more electromagnetic stimulation is extremely challenging for your eyes and your brain. It makes it hard for you to settle down and to sleep. If you're like most overworked, plugged-in adults, there are already many things that can potentially keep you awake and interrupt your sleep, creating physical challenges. The careless or automatic impulse to look at a screen right before bed is one of the worst, but also one of the easiest to avoid. We all need to stop screen usage half an hour before bed to get reasonable sleep. Binge watching is keeping us and our teens up late, and our adult brains are not exempt from those stressors.[2] For me, it's helpful to combine simple habits, anchoring a habit I do reliably, like brushing my teeth, with one that might be a little harder to accomplish, like turning off screens. I do

> We all need to stop screen usage half an hour before bed to get reasonable sleep.

them both at the same time, so I usually put down or turn off screens before I brush my teeth. Of course, I don't eat again after brushing, so I don't pick up the screen or open the computer again before sleeping. Or even simpler: Just as you want to clean your teeth before bed, it's good to remember to clean your mind before you sleep. You may have your own quick list for mind cleansing, but if not, here's mine. I take five or ten minutes for any one of the following: prayer, meditation, deep breathing, listening to classical or relaxing music, tai chi, positive thoughts, reflecting on my day with gratitude, diffusing essential oils like lavender, smiling. There are many strategies, but they only work when you *do* them.

> Just as you want to clean your teeth before bed, it's good to remember to clean your mind before you sleep.

From Recreational Therapy to Compulsion

Long before binge watching was "a thing," I knew adults who had challenged the onset of depression or had gotten through a looming nervous breakdown by watching every episode of *West Wing*. On International Children's Media Center (ICMC) programs like *World-Scene* and *Global Girls*, I've witnessed how powerful and cathartic films can be. I know several therapists who use films in therapeutic contexts with their clients.

We (and sometimes our children) can also gain relief from seeing screen content that mirrors our experiences, especially if we're feeling shamed or intimidated and feel we need to hide or deny those experiences. It can help to know that we're not "the only ones" to have those experiences because it means that we're not alone in facing those life challenges. For children, an unpleasant event like getting yelled at by a neighbor, breaking something accidentally, or getting lost at an amusement park can be challenging and can catalyze more fear, guilt, and self-doubt than they can first express. When a child sees that same event happen to a character in a movie or television show, it becomes more normative and neutral, so they don't feel different.

Watching films, TV, and short videos or playing with our favorite apps can open our minds in new directions, or relieve them so we can heal ourselves from our own stressors. Whether the purpose is entertainment or stress relief, it's fine to relax and "veg out" from time to time. Just balance couch-potato viewing or "sleep watching" so that it doesn't stretch indefinitely into a habit that steals your time and invades your neural territories with templates for behaviors or beliefs that you don't truly hold.

That said, I think we're all aware that there's a dark side to binge watching and nonstop screen use, aka screen addiction. As we stand at the gateway to artificial intelligence and neural implants, it may be useful to reflect on the fact that the creators of apps, games, and social media software are completely aware of the addictive lures of their products and embed them intentionally. Nir Eyal, author of *Hooked: How to Build Habit-Forming Products,* is unapologetic about the compulsions these products create. He justifies them as the result of a creative market economy, while at the same time recommending products and apps to neutralize their lures and protect his family. Some of Eyal's favorites include a Chrome extension called DF (for distraction free) YouTube that "scrubs" a lot of external triggers, an app called Pocket Points that rewards students for staying off their phones during class, and an outlet timer that cuts off access to the Internet at specific times.[3] Building a digital levee to hold back the rising tide of devices, apps, games, and content offers some protection, but only if we also teach our children to turn on their minds before turning on the screen. Using screens with purpose, communication, and self-awareness provides a better developmental boost and preparation for life in a digital world.

In 2017, Anderson Cooper interviewed Tristan Harris, now a Silicon Valley critic and a former product manager at Google, for CBS. During the interview, Harris referred to "the game" of the Internet and social media as a "race to the bottom of the brainstem."[4] Harris is another of the group of developers and tech insiders now sounding warnings about the ethical and actual dangers of technology, games, and social media. In this fascinating about-face, the story coming from these "tech heretics" now matches the stories coming from pediatricians, parents, and teachers. Groups that drew battle lines now share a rising common ground that can offer the perspective and elevation to help us *change the way we use digital devices.*[5] That's the solution I've been offering throughout this book. Being Screen Smart creates community around screens and leads us to use them less frequently but with greater purpose. Noticing and talking about our responses makes us more self-aware and less likely to overindulge. Including screen time in family discourse creates new bonds and big gains in literacy and empathy. While I'm grateful to see tech developers speaking out, this is the same wake-up call that we've heard for decades and Screen Smart skills are a crucial part of the awakening.

Cherishing the Choice
to Pay Attention

In any culture, but especially in a media-driven digital culture, we need to affirm our fundamental freedoms of reflection, choice, and selection. As an adult, those freedoms rest on my choosing what I allow into my mind and being aware of how I'm influenced. Knowing I have a choice is a good first step. In fact, my primary power over myself and my digital world lies in my ability to notice what's getting into my mind and how I'm responding to it. I don't know about you, but I really don't want to give up that power.

Experimenting, testing yourself, and pushing the envelope containing that power are all valid steps on the path of maturation. But whether you're trying mind-altering substances, extreme sports, or trekking Everest, the point is to notice what strengthens rather than penalizes your mind and mood. If you notice that whatever you've tried makes your mind sluggish, that it induces paranoia, or that your productivity declines to such a degree that you're sliding toward job termination, then it's good to reassess. But that capacity for self-awareness, reflection, assessment, and action has to be valued and honored in the twenty-first century—not just handed over to machines. We are the upside of digital devices. It is our humanity, our shared experiences, our capacity for change and compassion that can harness the power of these electronic tools for the greatest personal and collective good. That's a twenty-first century story worth sharing and creating together.

Appendix

Good Books About Screen Time

Borba, Michele. *Unselfie: Why Empathetic Kids Succeed in Our All-About-Me World.* New York, NY: Touchstone, 2017.

Dr. Borba's book provides parents with a research-based, nine-step program for guiding your child toward becoming a kinder and more empathetic person. Her program is clear and concise, and delves deep into specific strategies for helping your child become the best they can be.

Calvert, Sandra, and Wilson, Barbara. *The Handbook of Children, Media and Development.* New Jersey: Wiley-Blackwell, 2008.

For the academically inclined, this book provides an authoritative and thorough overview of the research being done today on digital media and its influence on child development.

Donohue, Chip. *Family Engagement in the Digital Age: Early Childhood Educators as Media Mentors.* London: Rutledge Taylor & Francis, 2017.

Chip Donohue, PhD, is the Director of the TEC (Technology in Early Childhood) Center at the Erikson Institute. His book serves as a guide to best practices for educators and parents for becoming media mentors to young children.

Dunckley, Victoria L. *Reset Your Child's Brain: A Four-Week Plan to End Meltdowns, Raise Grades, and Boost Social Skills by Reversing the Effects of Electronic Screen-Time.* Novato, CA: New World Library, 2015.

Dr. Victoria Dunckley develops palliative techniques for children diagnosed with disorders often associated with screen addiction. The book presents a four-week program to overcome "electronic screen syndrome" and reverse its deleterious effects on our children's emotional, social, and neural growth.

Eyal, Nir. *Hooked: How to Build Habit-Forming Products.* New York, NY. Penguin: 2014.

Eyal masterfully explains the Hook Model—a four-step process companies use in their products to influence customer behavior. The book provides answers to questions such as "Why am I addicted to this technology?" "What makes us use this product habitually?"

Guernsey, Lisa. *Screen Time: How Electronic Media—From Baby Videos to Educational Software—Affects Your Young Child.* Philadelphia, PA: Basic Books, 2007.

Journalist Lisa Guernsey, mother of two, investigates for herself the influences of electronic media on children. Her book provides straight answers and practical advice for all parents wondering about the effects of their kids' screen time.

Heitner, Devorah. *Screenwise: Helping Kids Thrive (and Survive) in Their Digital World.* Brookline, MA: Bibliomotion Incorporated, 2016.

Written for parents who recognize the potential of technology to empower their ten-year-old to tween children but are unclear about how to guide them. "Screenwise" lays out helpful parenting "hacks" and offers insightful anecdotes from parents with similar struggles.

Kardaras, Nicholas. *Glow Kids: How Screen Addiction Is Hijacking Our Kids— and How to Break the Trance.* New York, NY: St. Martin's Press, 2017.

An in-depth look at the effects of screens on children, this book focuses more on what is going on in the brain of a child who is addicted to screens. It provides a robust, albeit one-sided, counterargument to those who advocate for the educational potential of screens and technology.

Kamenetz, Anya. *The Art of Screen Time: How Your Family Can Balance Digital Media and Real Life.* New York, NY: Public Affairs Hachette Book Group, 2018.

Anya Kamenetz, education author and head education blogger at NPR combed through hundreds of parent surveys and scientific studies to craft a compelling, yet simple philosophy about finding balance between screen time and direct experience.

Minow, Nell. *The Movie Mom's Guide to Family Movies.* Lincoln, NE: iUniverse Inc., 2004.

Now in its second edition, Minow's guide is a wonderful reference for parents sitting down to decide what to watch with their family, complete with descriptions specifically written for parents.

Palladino, Lucy Jo. *Parenting in the Age of Attention Snatchers: A Step-by-Step Guide to Balancing Your Child's Use of Technology.* Boston, MA: Shambhala, 2015.

Palladino's book gives parents seven straightforward steps on how to teach their kids to cultivate control over their attention—both voluntary and involuntary.

Tsabary, Shefali. *The Conscious Parent: Transforming Ourselves, Empowering Our Children.* London, UK: Yellow Kite, 2014.

This book is a departure from the pervasive "know it all" approach to parenting in our society. Tsabary advocates for a more conscious and present parenting style, while giving clever strategies for dismantling dysfunction and maintaining control over your child's development.

Twenge, Jean M. *IGen: Why Today's Super-Connected Kids Are Growing Up Less Rebellious, More Tolerant, Less Happy—and Completely Unprepared for Adulthood and What That Means for the Rest of Us.* New York, NY: Atria Books, 2017.

From the author of *Generation Me*, this book explores the causes of generational divides and offers ways to gain common ground. For parents this serves as a practical guide on relating to children who have grown up never knowing life without a smart phone.

Organizations You May Find Helpful

Although these are not the only organizations and websites offering resources to parents, these are, in my view, some of the best, complementing those of **Common Sense Media**. commonsensemedia.org

The American Academy of Pediatrics Family Media Plan helps chart media use and trace healthy/unhealthy habits in regard to media consumption. healthychildren.org/English/media/Pages/default.aspx

Center on Media and Child Health (CMCH) is based at Harvard and focused on health and development in a media-rich environment. Their primary goal is to help children consume media in ways that will optimize their development. cmch.tv

The Center for Media Literacy is working to promote critical thinking and media literacy throughout the nation. They have some effective, parent-friendly approaches for talking to children about commercials and how to end the "buy me that" tantrums. medialit.org

The Children's Digital Media Center is a group of scholars located across the nation dedicated to the study of how digital media influences child development. cdmc.george town.edu

The Fred Rogers Center, founded in 2003 at Saint Vincent College in Latrobe, Pennsylvania, is devoted to continuing Rogers' legacy of enriching the lives of young children through the developmentally appropriate use of media. fredrogerscenter.org/

The International Children's Media Center's mission is to help children use screens in healthy ways that boost literacy, learning, and empathy. ICMC's neuroscience-based programs for parents, teachers, and children are offered in schools, community centers, libraries, universities, shelters, and hospitals. icmediacenter.org

The Joan Ganz Cooney Center is dedicated to advancing children's learning in a digital age. The Center works with policymakers and investors to help steer the national conversation on media and education. Joanganzcooneycenter.org

Kids-In-Mind. Movie ratings created with parents in mind. Although congested with ads, this is a detailed resource for making sure a movie is appropriate for your child. kids-in-mind.com

LeVar Burton Kids. The host of PBS' wildly popular *Reading Rainbow*, LeVar Burton's website and Skybrary app focus on stimulating kids' curiosity and critical thinking. levarburtonkids.com

Tap, Click, Read. Lisa Guernsey's website and book is dedicated to growing readers in a world of screens. Guernsey's tips and toolkits are an excellent resource. tapclickread.org

Although more specifically geared toward early childhood classroom teachers, the **Erikson Institute's Technology in Early Childhood Center (TEC)** is a strong proponent of addressing the need for more responsible and effective use of technology in early childhood settings. teccenter.erikson.edu/

Acronyms Used in This Book

AI	Artificial Intelligence
APA	American Psychological Association
EI	Emotional Intelligence
ELMO	Enough Let's Move On
ESS	Electronic Screen Syndrome
FBSS	Fun Bad Sad Scary
ICMC	International Children's Media Center
NAEYC	National Association for the Education of Young Children
P&Q	Pause and Question
PAT	Parent Attention Time
SEL	Social and Emotional Learning
VR	Virtual Reality
ZPD	Zone of Proximal Development

Endnotes

Chapter 1

[1] Patricia McDonough. "TV Viewing Among Kids at an Eight-Year High." The Nielsen Company (2009.) http://www.nielsen.com/us/en/insights/news/2009/tv-viewing-among-kids-at-an-eight-year-high.html

[2] Useful books on active listening:

Adele Faber and Elaine Mazlish. *How to Talk So Kids Will Listen and Listen So Kids Will Talk.* New York, NY: Scribner, 2012.

Adele Faber and Elaine Mazlish. *Liberated Parents, Liberated Children: Your Guide to a Happier Family.* New York, NY: Harper, 2004.

Thomas Gordon. *Parent Effectiveness Training: The Proven Program for Raising Responsible Children.* New York, NY: Three Rivers Press, 2000.

Daniel J. Siegel and Tina Payne Bryson. *No-Drama Discipline: The Whole-Brain Way to Calm the Chaos and Nurture Your Child's Developing Mind.* New York, NY: Bantam Books, 2016.

[3] "Talk time" between caregiver and child remains critical for language development. Passive video presentations do not lead to language learning in infants and young toddlers. The more media engender live interactions, the more educational value they may hold. (Brown, 2015)

Ari Brown, Donald L. Shifrin, and David L. Hill. "Beyond 'turn it off': How to advise families on media use." *AAP News* 36 (2015).

Chapter 2

[1] Daschell M. Phillips, "Films at Koz: Program at Kozminski puts films into focus," *Hyde Park Herald* Vol. 132, Issue 25: 1–2.

Chapter 4

[1] Some sources describing the importance of nonverbal communication:

Albert Mehrabian. *Nonverbal Communication.* Piscataway, NJ: Transaction Publishers, 1972.

Geoffrey Beattie. *Visible Thoughts: The New Psychology of Body Language.* Hove, East Sussex: Routledge, 2003.

Antonietta Trimboli and Michael B. Walker. "Nonverbal Dominance in the Communication of Affect: A Myth?" *Journal of Nonverbal Behavior* 11 (1987): 180–190.

[2] Here are some brief tips for scaffolding children's learning:

- ❖ Select a challenge that is just beyond what your child can already do easily by him or herself.
- ❖ Describe it in simple language.
- ❖ Give cues or prompts.
- ❖ Ask questions.
- ❖ Model the actions or steps involved.
- ❖ Praise your child for undertaking the task, not just for succeeding.

Guided participation is when we assist children as they perform grown-up or more mature activities. Scaffolding occurs when teachers, parents or those who have the competency being taught provide some form of structure or guidance that enables children to perform tasks at their zone of proximal development.

Lev S. Vygotsky, *The Problem and The Approach*. Cambridge, MA: Massachusetts Institute of Technology Press, 2012.

Chapter 5

[1] Marc Bornstein, head of child and family research at the National Institute of Child Health and Human Development, along with Martha Arterberry, professor of psychology at Colby College, worked together to create their published work of studies in "Developmental Psychology" to explain the importance of exposing children to object categories.

"Categories are especially valuable in infancy and early childhood when many new objects, events, and people are encountered because, without the ability and proclivity to categorize, children would have to learn to respond anew to each novel entity they experience" (Bornstein, Arterberry).

Generally speaking, categories mediate our interactions with the world (Smith, 1989) insofar as they structure and clarify perception and cognition (Bornstein, 1984; Harnad, 1987). The environment affords an infinite variety of stimulation and is incessantly changing. Moreover, we experience the world out of a constant biological flux. Both these major sources of variation must be reduced if perception and cognition are to proceed with organization, order, and coherence."

Bornstein, Marc H., and Martha E. Arterberry. "The Development of Objects Categorization in Young Children: Hierarchal Inclusiveness, Age, Perceptual Attribute, and Group Versus Individual Analyses." *Developmental psychology* 46.2 (2010): 350–365. *PMC.*

Chapter 6

[1] John Grinder and Richard Bandler. *Frogs into Princes: Neuro Linguistic Programming*. Moab, UT: Real People Press, 1980.

[2] Dominic W. Massaro. "Two Different Communication Genres and Implications for Vocabulary Development and Learning to Read." *Journal of Literacy Research* 47 (2015): 505–27.

Chapter 7

[1] Lisa Guernsey. *Screen Time: How Electronic Media—From Baby Videos to Educational Software—Affects Your Young Child.* Philadelphia, PA: Basic Books, 2007.

[2] Victoria L. Dunckley. *Reset Your Child's Brain: A Four-Week Plan to End Meltdowns, Raise Grades, and Boost Social Skills by Reversing the Effects of Electronic Screen-Time.* Novato, CA: New World Library, 2015.

[3] Sandra Bond Chapman. *Make Your Brain Smarter.* New York, NY: Simon and Schuster, 2013.

[4] Betsy Wallace. (2003, August 04). *Friends—TV* Review. Retrieved September 20, 2017, from www.commonsensemedia.org/tv-reviews/friends

[5] Here are a few additional books that have solid scripts to support talking about sex:

Laura Berman. *Talking to Your Kids about Sex: Turning "The Talk" into a Conversation for Life.* New York, NY: DK Publications, 2009.

Laurie Krasny Brown. *What's the Big Secret? Talking about Sex with Girls and Boys.* New York, NY: Little, Brown and Company, 2000.

Sandra E. Byers, et al. "Parents' Reports of Sexual Communication with Children in Kindergarten to Grade 8." *Journal of Marriage and Family* 70 (2008): 86–96.

[6] Tara Bahrampour. 'There Isn't Really Anything Magical About It': Why More Millennials Are Avoiding Sex." *The Washington Post,* Aug. 2, 2016, https://www.washingtonpost.com/local/social-issues/there-isnt-really-anything-magical-about-it-why-more-millennials-are-putting-off-sex/2016/08/02/e7b73d6e-37f4-11e6-8f7c-d4c723a2becb_story.html?utm_term=.02cd3ca76b7f

Wendy Wang and Kim Parker. "Record Share of Americans Have Never Married." Pew Research Center Social and Demographic Trends, Pew Research Center, 24 Sept. 2014, http://www.pewsocialtrends.org/2014/09/24/record-share-of-americans-have-never-married/#will-todays-never-married-adults-eventually-marry

"I Don't—Marriage in Japan." *The Economist,* Sept. 3, 2016, https://www.economist.com/news/asia/21706321-most-japanese-want-be-married-are-finding-it-hard-i-dont

Kaori Shoji. "Women in Japan Too Tired to Care About Dating or Searching for a Partner." *The Japan Times,* Dec. 2, 2017, https://www.japantimes.co.jp/news/2017/12/02/national/media-national/women-tired-care-dating-searching-partner/#.WoHKEmVsyhY

Chapter 8

[1] Dr. George Gerbner, the founder of the Cultural Indicators Project did seminal research that is still relevant despite being confined to television. The proliferation of screens may add more species of electronic trees to the digital forest, but the underlying structures and root systems remain consistent. Decades before Harari, Gerbner made many of the same statements and for a different purpose. Gerbner wanted us to remain aware that those who are controlling the flow of stories have more to sell than to tell.

"Human beings are unique to other species in that we live in a world that is created by the stories we tell. Most of what we know, or think we know, we have never personally experienced; we learned about it through stories."

Scott Stossel. "The Man Who Counts the Killings." *The Atlantic Monthly* 279 (1997): 86–104.

[2] Yuval Noah Harari. *Sapiens*. New York, NY: HarperCollins, 2015.

[3] Betty Hart & Todd R. Risley "The Early Catastrophe: The 30 Million Word Gap by Age 3." *American Educator* 27(2003): 4–9

Chapter 9

[1] It may seem counterintuitive to use physical energy prior to screen use, but research shows that the value of exercise and movement aligns with the improvements of cognitive skills and mental capacity. When children release their energy with the proper use of exercise in combination with cognitive tasks the body generates the best capabilities in processing and memory.

Phillip D. Tomporowski et al. "Exercise and Children's Intelligence, Cognition, and Academic Achievement." *Educational psychology review* 20.2 (2008): 111–131. PMC. Web. Aug. 28, 2017.

Timothy J. Schoenfeld, et al. "Physical Exercise Prevents Stress-Induced Activation of Granule Neurons and Enhances Local Inhibitory Mechanisms in the Dentate Gyrus." *Journal of Neuroscience* 33 (2013): 7770–7777.

Laura Chaddock-Heyman, et al. "The Role of Aerobic Fitness in Cortical Thickness and Mathematics Achievement in Preadolescent Children." *Plos One* 10 (2015).

Larry A. Tucker. "Physical Activity and Telomere Length in U.S. Men and Women: An NHANES Investigation." *Preventive Medicine* 100 (2017): 145–151.

[2] In 2015 in Taiwan, a young man identified as Hsieh was found sprawled on a table at an Internet café, where he'd spent three straight days gaming (Hunt, 2015). Hsieh died from cardiac failure as a result of cold temperatures and over-exhaustion after a three-day gaming binge (Hunt, 2015). The same type of horrendous event occurred in Russia the same year.

Katie Hunt and Naomi Ng. "Man Dies in Taiwan After 3-Day Online Gaming Binge." *CNN* (2015).

C. Shu-ting and W. Po-hsuan. "Gamers Ignore Corpse in Internet Café." *Taipei Times* (2014).

M. Morrow. "Russian Teenager Dies After Playing Online Computer Game 'Defence of the Ancients' for 22 Days in a Row." *News Corp Australia Network* (2015).

Chapter 10

[1] Tenzin Gyatso. *Ancient Wisdom, Modern World: Ethics for the New Millennium*. London, UK: Abacus, 1999.

[2] Instead of just extolling the virtues of 3 TB hard drives and exponentially powerful processors, it can be a joy to re-acquaint ourselves with the power of the human brain.

Joe Dispenza. *You Are the Placebo: Making Your Mind Matter*. Carlsbad, CA: Hay House Inc., 2015.

Carl Zimmer. "100 Trillion Connections: New Efforts Probe and Map the Brain's Detailed Architecture." *Scientific American* 304 (2011): 58-63.

"Your Brain Is Still 30 Times More Powerful than the Best Supercomputers" Last modified August 28, 2015. https://www.sciencealert.com/your-brain-is-still-30-times-more-powerful-than-the-best-supercomputers

"How Powerful Is the Human Brain Compared to a Computer?" Last modified March 2, 2016. www.forbes.com/sites/akamai/2017/09/14/identifying-hazards-to-better-prepare-for-cyber attacks/#2ad7a2252be7

[3] Walter Mischel. *The Marshmallow Test: Mastering Self-Control.* New York, NY: Little, Brown and Company, 2014.

Chapter 12

[1] Eddie Brummelman, et al. "Origins of Narcissism in Children." *Proceedings of the National Academy of Sciences* 112 (2015): 3659–3662

[2] Children who are healthy and successful in their cognitive and social-emotional development have much greater chances of becoming productive and engaged citizens, making positive contributions in society, and elevating the level of overall population health. (Cooper et al., 2011).

[3] Global estimates of the number and percentage of children with low cognitive and/or socioemotional development [...] suggest that 80.8 million 3- and 4-y-old children [...] experienced low cognitive and/or socioemotional development in 2010 as measured by the "Early Childhood Development Index" (McCoy et al, 2016).

D.C. McCoy, et al. "Early Childhood Developmental Status in Low- and Middle-Income Countries: National, Regional, and Global Prevalence Estimates Using Predictive Modeling." *PLoS Med* 13(2016).

D. E. Jones, M. Greenberg and M. Crowley. "Early Social-Emotional Functioning and Public Health: The Relationship Between Kindergarten Social Competence and Future Wellness." *American Journal of Public Health*, 105(2015), 2283–2290.

Chapter 13

[1] Sherry Turkle. *Reclaiming Conversation: The Power of Talk in a Digital Age.* New York, NY: Penguin Books, 2017.

Chapter 14

[1] Here, I think it's worthwhile to look at the broad range of research that encourages minimal use of digital devices between ages eighteen months and five years. Each hour of average daily television viewing before age three years was associated with deleterious effects on [...the] Reading Recognition Scale [...the] Reading Comprehension Scale and on the Memory for Digit Span. (Zimmerman, 2005)

L. Alessio. "Handheld Screen Time Linked to Delayed Speech Development." *ASHA Leader* 22 (2017): 16.

According to Tomopolous, language development in young children is being hindered by excessive media exposure. (Tomopolous, 2010)

S. Tomopoulos, et al. "Infant Media Exposure and Toddler Development" *Archives of Pediatrics & Adolescent Medicine* 164 (2010).

A. L. Mendelsohn. "Infant Media Exposure and Toddler Development." *Archives of Pediatrics & Adolescent Medicine* 164 (2010): 1105–1111.

Sarah Knapton. "Tablets and Smartphones Damage Toddlers' Speech Development." *The Telegraph* (2017).

V. Mohney. (2017, May 5). "Handheld Screen Use in Toddlers Linked to Speech Delays, Study Finds." Retrieved from http://abcnews.go.com/Health/handheld-screen-toddlers-linked-speech-delays-study-finds/story?id=47203699

[2] Exelmans and J. Van den Bulck, "Binge Viewing, Sleep, and the Role of Pre-Sleep Arousal." *J Clin Sleep Med.* 13 (2017):1001–1008.

[3] Paul Lewis. "'Our Minds Can Be Hijacked': The Tech Insiders Who Fear a Smartphone Dystopia." *The Guardian*, October 6, 2017.

[4] Anderson Cooper. "What Is 'Brain Hacking'? Tech Insiders on Why You Should Care." *CBS News*, CBS Interactive, Apr. 9, 2017, www.cbsnews.com/news/brain-hacking-tech-insiders-60-minutes/.

[5] Bianca Bosker. "The Binge Breaker: Tristan Harris Believes Silicon Valley Is Addicting Us to Your Phones. He's Determined to Make It Stop." *The Atlantic*, November 2016).